SECRETS and LIES

Also by Jane Isay

Walking on Eggshells
Mom Still Likes You Best

SECRETS and LIES

Surviving the Truths That
Change Our Lives

Jane Isay

DOUBLEDAY

New York   London   Toronto
Sydney   Auckland

www.doubleday.com

DOUBLEDAY and the portrayal of an anchor with a dolphin
are registered trademarks of Random House LLC.

Book design by Michael Collica
Jacket design by Emily Mahon
Jacket illustration: drape: © Mike Harrington/Photodisc/Getty Images;
family: © Tetra Images/Alamy; frame: © Niels Poulsen DK/Alamy

Library of Congress Cataloging-in-Publication Data
Isay, Jane.
Secrets and lies : Surviving the truths that change our lives /
Jane Isay.
pages   cm
1. Gay fathers.   2. Closeted gays.   3. Family secrets.
4. Families.   5. Deception.   I. Title.
HQ76.13.I83 2014
306.85—dc23
2013018902

ISBN 978-0-385-53414-7

MANUFACTURED IN THE UNITED STATES OF AMERICA

1 3 5 7 9 10 8 6 4 2

First Edition

For Benjamin, Ruby, Tobey, Mazie
My love for you is no secret

CONTENTS

INTRODUCTION: FINDERS, KEEPERS

The pain of learning a secret
and the price of keeping it

This is a book about the secrets that change our lives. When we learn a secret that someone we love has been keeping from us, our sense of reality is shaken. We begin to question our memories, our experiences, and our expectations.

Secrets and Lies delves into the rage and the misery and hopelessness we feel when we learn a secret that has betrayed our trust. It's about the deep and powerful urges we have to maintain the status quo despite the secrets we hold to ourselves. It's about the need we have to stay connected to the people we have wronged by our secrets and the people who have wronged us by hiding the truth from us. It's about our need for honesty and our desire for reconciliation. It's about our mistakes and our desire to make amends. When an important secret is revealed, our world changes. We may ask ourselves: Who am I? Who is this stranger? Why did this happen to me, and why was it hidden? Who can I trust, and what kind of a fool have I been? How can I live my life now that I know the truth?

I have experienced all of these feelings and more, and so have many of the people whose stories you will read in this book. You'll learn about secrets that transform our identity: you were adopted; your father isn't really dead. You'll read stories about secrets that destroy trust: a man discovers that his wife has been sleeping with the teenage babysitter. There are secrets that people have been urged to keep for the sake of the family: a sister died at ten; a father committed suicide—it wasn't pneumonia after all.

Discovering that someone you love has lied to you and kept a secret feels like being hit by a bolt of lightning. Such is the circumstance of the Finder, the person to whom the truth is revealed. The arc of his or her life is altered in an instant. Everything that has been planned and expected fades away. Suddenly the present makes no sense and the future is impossible to picture. Why are these revelations so devastating? What difference does a new turn in the plot of our lives make?

As human beings, we live the stories we tell ourselves. This internal narrative makes up the core of our identity. Every day, and in every circumstance, we tell and retell our story. As we encounter new information, the story adjusts a little bit. It is altered as we move through life. Think of our stories as a set of movies. Some are about our origins—who we come from and how we were formed—so finding out information that changes the story is shocking. For example, learning that you are not your parents' child shakes you to the core. Other stories enable us to live our lives as adults. They are about who we love and how we live. When a husband who has been cheating on you for years finally blurts out the truth, your reality is transformed in a flash. Others are about the future. How can you handle a side of the family you never knew existed?

In order to make wise decisions we project a series of scenarios. We mentally—and often unconsciously—plan and play out events as if we were the stars of our own movie. We make our choices based on our preference for one or another of the scenarios we create. When a secret is revealed, the movies of our lives are shredded. The film has jumped its sprockets. How and when do we reclaim our reality and tell ourselves a new story that is more faithful to the truth? When our reality is fragmented, so are we.

The secret keeper, the person who has a truth so shameful that it must be hidden, is also pained by the difference between reality and appearance. The Keeper will shape her responses to the appearance of things, not to her genuine feelings. The Keeper will become constantly alert in order to keep contradictions— and intimacy—at bay. It becomes easy to lie about why you got home late, or who was on the phone. That is the life of the secret keeper. Fragmentation is the rule. Honesty and closeness are the enemy. How can you live with yourself and with people you love while you are keeping a secret about your sister or your child or yourself, and why would you do it?

Is it shame? Is it commitment to the status quo? Is it fear of retribution or rejection?

The Keeper suffers self-doubt and worries about the future.

How can you square the deception with your desire to be a good person? How would your life change if the truth came out?

The Keeper worries about being found out. The Keeper needs

to walk fast and talk fast around the truth. It's a hard job. The Keeper also tries to create an internal story that keeps self-judgment at bay, because as human beings we don't like to see ourselves as bad people. So we rationalize, and we explain, and we cover over the bright shiny truth. We tell ourselves stories about how much better off everybody is if they are ignorant. The Keeper is afraid of change, of retribution, and of being judged.

Sometimes events intervene. An anonymous letter appears, or a lost relative turns up at a family funeral. A piece of paper falls out of a wallet, or a secret diary is read for the first time. Sometimes the Keeper can no longer bear the conflict between telling lies and being a person worthy of self-respect. So a confession is made.

Now comes the hard part: to face and reconcile to the new reality. Here both the Finder and the Keeper have choices. Do you tell your adult daughter why you adopted her and kept it a secret? Do you sit through the recriminations that follow the revelation of lies told over decades?

The Finder may dissolve into rage and grief and sever the relationship. The Finder may decide to ignore the truth and move on as if nothing happened. The Finder may struggle and fail to integrate the new truth into the life story. Or the Finder may decide to create a livable reality that includes the truth.

Integrating that new reality and living with it takes work, and people have many ways of accomplishing this, as you will see in the pages that follow.

If the Keeper wants to repair and maintain relationships

with the people who have been misled and betrayed, hard work lies ahead, including:

a full confession of all the facts
an explanation of the reasons for the secret
acceptance of responsibility for the betrayal
repentance without rationalization
the patience to rebuild

You may wonder why I write with such conviction about the crises and pain that secrets cause. I have interviewed more than sixty people who have told me stories of the secrets they have carried and the secrets they have learned. But before I even began the interviews, I was already an expert.

I lived as both a Finder and a Keeper for much of the last half century. My story is about thunderbolts and denial. It's about love and sorrow. It's about the power that secrets have to attract and repel. It's about the damage we suffer when we hide the truth.

A Love Story

I grew up in a time when medical school graduates often took what they called rotating internships, moving from specialty to specialty over their first year as physicians. The summer after my sophomore year in college I rotated young doctors—dating four different specialties: On Monday I went out with the ophthalmologist; Tuesday was the ear, nose, and throat specialist; internal medicine was Wednesday; and Thursday was rehabilitative medicine. My mother was determined that I marry a doctor, for both historical and practical reasons. I had not fallen in love yet, and so I serially dated these nice young doctors all week and went upstate on Fridays to spend the weekends at the house my parents rented. At summer's end I went back to college and the young doctors moved on with their lives. This dating pattern continued for the rest of my college years. Sometimes I would sneak a young lawyer into the rotation—just to be rebellious.

Some of these men proposed marriage. One of them started to propose in an elevator going down from his high-rise apartment in Philadelphia, but was interrupted when somebody got on at the eighth floor. It was weird. I hardly knew these men and I couldn't imagine why they would want to marry me. Either it was for sex, which in those days demanded a long-term commitment, or because they found me attractive and from a suitable family. I liked them fine, but there was no spark, and I turned each of them down. That was the dating career of a proper young woman who followed the rules.

After college I went to graduate school. My parents were still looking for a doctor to marry me when they fixed me up with the son of a famous physician, a young man in medical school, on my first Christmas break. I opened the door of the apartment and before me was an adorable, dark-eyed man in a black Chesterfield coat. Jonathan. He took me to a revue at the Plaza Hotel, *Upstairs at the Downstairs*. We loved it. It was lightly snowing as we walked down Fifth Avenue to the Christmas tree in Rockefeller Center, and by the time we finished our hot toddies at Reuben's, Jonathan and I were in love.

This was different. Our connection was instant and passionate. Within days, we had decided to marry in two years, when he finished medical school. In honor of our relationship, his parents gave me a beautiful gold pin, flecked with rubies and diamonds. My mother and I rode in a taxicab around Central Park planning the wedding (pink, at the Pierre), and then I went back to school. Jonathan and I spoke every day, racking up enormous long-distance telephone bills. He came to visit once, and we wrote daily. As the spring drew on, his letters took on a tone of sadness. He hated medical school, and he was not doing well. His parents had urged this career on him, even though he fainted at the sight of blood and found his studies a bore. He was a reader, a literary person, not a scientist. The clouds were gathering for both of us. I disliked graduate school and realized that a PhD was not for me, so I decided to drop out.

When I got home that May, Jonathan announced that he was quitting medical school. He had not prepared anybody for his decision. He had indicated his unhappiness to me, but he was not up-front with his parents or with mine. He kept it a secret because he knew what a disappointment his decision would be. I'm not sure he expected the disaster that ensued.

My parents told me to break off the engagement. I mustn't marry a liar. He had wooed me under false pretenses. They were adamant. My father was a psychiatrist and dean of a rabbinical school in New York, and my mother wrote an advice column in the *New York Post*. I couldn't stand up to them. I realized that life in New York would be hard without their support. I knew that my parents' disapproval would cast a pall over our relationship. So I invited him to the apartment. "I can't go ahead with this," I said. "We can't get married. It isn't working." He flushed with anger. "You just couldn't buck them, could you?" he said, as he motioned his head toward my parents' side of the apartment. I nodded as I handed him a check for the money he had advanced me to pay my long-distance phone bill. His head was bowed as he pocketed the check and walked out the door. It was the worst thing I have ever done to another person.

Just as we were going through the breakup, I got a call from one of the sophomore-summer doctors. Honestly, I wasn't sure which one he was, perhaps the ophthalmologist, perhaps the ear, nose, and throat specialist? I did recognize the name, Dick, and he sounded nice. He was calling from New Haven and asked if I was free the next weekend. I couldn't do it. The breakup was too fresh. I said I was busy, and when he called again a week later, I offered the same excuse. There was a pause. I felt I had to tell him the truth, that I was breaking up a serious relationship and was not ready to date anybody. I'd let him know, I promised, when things were calmer.

A month or so later, I dropped him a note. He called the next week to make a date. The day came, the bell rang, I opened the door, and it was the tall, handsome, Rusk intern, now a resident in psychiatry—at Yale. Dick and I started dating, this time for real. He was lovely, fun to be with, kind, smart, with a quirky sense of humor, and a serious reader. That he was tall, extremely handsome, and came from a good family didn't hurt. I think my parents fell in love with him before I did. Dick's father had died when he was a kid, and he connected immediately with my father, whom he loved. My formidable mother, the psychologist Rose N. Franzblau, was a little intimidated by my Yale psychiatrist, which pleased me no end.

We dated for more than a year. After the intensity of Jonathan I appreciated Dick's coolness. He would drive to New York, and I would visit him in New Haven. We always had a good time when we went to dinner or the theater, and there was something a little mysterious about him. He would retreat from intimacy in a way that piqued my interest. It was a change from the old days—now I was the one who did the pursuing, and that offered a challenge. He was a true gentleman during our courtship. We slept in the same room—Dick on his pullout couch and me on a pullout chair. He never made a move. I liked his respectful attitude. Then one weekend we drove down to Philadelphia to meet his sister and her husband and their baby. That night, in the hotel, we made love, and Dick proposed to me in the car on the way home. We informed my parents, who could not have been more delighted.

His mother, grandmother, and sister came to New York and we met. Just as I sat down on the couch in their hotel room, Dick's mom pulled a jewelry bag from her purse and gave it to me. It was a necklace made of many strings of baby pearls wound around each other. The sophomore summer when we had first met, Dick had told his mother that he had found the girl he was going to marry. His mother went to Hong Kong soon after and had bought the necklace to give to me—long before Dick and I reconnected and fell in love and became engaged. It felt preordained.

The wedding was lovely, and the next day I moved with Dick to New Haven, where we began to build our life together. I got a job at Yale University Press, and he finished his residency in psychiatry. The most important part of his day was his psychoanalytic session. I grew up in a family where everybody was in analysis (but me). Dick went six days a week, though, every week of the year, and that seemed intense. When he needed to fulfill his obligation to the navy (this was the era of the doctor's draft), he bugged the Department of the Navy, asking to be posted at the naval base in Groton, an hour's commute from New Haven. They finally agreed and assigned him there. It was so important to Dick because he was utterly serious about his analysis.

The demands of his residency program forced us to postpone our honeymoon. Six months after the wedding, we flew to Mexico City. It smelled something awful to me. I had no appetite and wanted to sleep. Fine food and serious sightseeing had been the plan, and Dick was disappointed that naps were more important to me than museums. My period had been a little late, but I hadn't paid any attention to that, until one evening Dick complained that he took me to the finest restaurants and I only ate the bread and butter. That night I had a dream that I was on a train ride lasting nine months and wasn't even packed. When I told my psychiatrist husband the dream, he said, "You think you're pregnant." I nodded, and we got on the next plane home. That was the beginning of parenthood.

It was exciting to be young marrieds in New Haven in those years. Dick was forging a brilliant career in psychoanalysis and I was a rising young editor, introducing the university press to psychiatry and child development, subjects they had never recognized, much less published. The senior Freudian psychoanalysts adopted us—Dick was their favorite and I might be their editor. We loved our life. We laughed together. Sometimes at scholarly lectures or pompous dinners we couldn't even look at each other lest we erupt in giggles. We'd snuggle in bed at night talking over the silly and the intriguing. I would rest my head against his armpit—we called it his crux. Sex was not a big part of our relationship. It didn't seem to matter. We were a great team, and our bond was strong. I loved him, and he loved me.

When we tried to get pregnant the second time, things were not so easy. We would start out fine, but then something would turn Dick off. He would want to go to sleep. It was disheartening. I couldn't understand why Dick wasn't attracted to me. Was I too fat? Was I too assertive? I tried to make sense of it. Maybe it was my pushy personality. Eventually we conceived our second son, and that pretty much brought an end to our sex life. Anyway, we had fun together, and we laughed a lot and had a good time. Dick reassured me, from his authority as a psychoanalyst, that people who were married more than a few years rarely made love. I believed him.

Then, when our younger son was about four and we had been married nearly nine years, Dick finished his psychoanalysis. Things began to change. His attention gradually shifted. He was so involved in his work, and I in mine, and we were so busy with the boys, that we were no longer as close. We both were too distracted to worry about it. I embarked on an affair just about the time Dick ended his analysis. Knowing that a man found me sexually attractive reaffirmed a part of me, but it didn't mean as much to me as my marriage did. The relationship never had a future, and that was part of the plan.

Then my career at Yale blew up in a hurtful way. Dick was supportive and encouraged me to take a good job in New York, even though it meant a two-hour commute each way. It was a rough time for both of us. Dick's mother died the week before I started the job and my mother died that September. We were in perpetual mourning. I was commuting from New Haven to New York with two small sons at home. Dick held the fort while I was away, and we were exhausted. During this time, I noticed changes in Dick's behavior. He started taking long walks in the evening. On vacations he didn't stay with me in the hotel after dinner—more walks. Odd stories about his trips emerged. I was confused, and so I checked it out with a friend. She agreed that he was distracted and seemed to be a fugitive at the dinner table and suggested that I reassure him that, whatever his secret, I could take it—and that I still loved him. I did that, to great effect.

Dick had risen to prominence in his field, and I was running

Basic Books, a major publisher in the behavioral and social sciences. We always went to the annual meetings of the American Psychiatric Association together. He presented papers and organized meetings, and I scouted authors and sold books. We were a power couple.

Then one night, at the end of a meeting in San Francisco, Dick was a little late coming back to our room from a party for the Gay Caucus of the APA. Of course he would be on the side of the minority—that's the kind of man he is, and I supported him one hundred percent. I peeked out of the room and heard the happy sounds of the party down the hall.

But when he came in, Dick looked anxious and sad.

"I have something to tell you," he said, as he sat down on my side of the bed. "I'm homosexual."

"You're what?"

"Yes," he began, "all the years in my analysis we tried to cure me, but it didn't work. After it was over, I found my desires couldn't be controlled."

He went on to tell me of trips to New York to gay movie houses and risky episodes in men's rooms. It could no longer be denied, and I needed to know. His friends in the Gay Caucus had urged him to come clean to me that night. After his confession, Dick went back to the party to tell his friends that he had done it. I headed to the bathroom.

Chilled to the bone, I ran the hottest bath I could manage and sank into the water. My skin prickled from the heat, but it did not warm me up. Everything that I had built my life on was in ruins. What would our future be? How could we survive this? When Dick got back to the room, we talked all night about his struggles and my worries.

I had taken my friend's advice and reassured him of my love, and I still loved him, but I was scared. So was Dick. We couldn't figure out our future. The Freudian circles where Dick was a star were severely homophobic. He couldn't come out as a gay man and be taken seriously. His career would be ruined. He didn't want to give up his family, and he loved me. I didn't want to give him up, or the family, or our place in society, or our financial security, and there was no taking back my love for him.

So as we flew home—sitting in the back of the plane, arms around each other, crying and talking—we tried to figure it out. By the time we landed in New York, we were clear: We would stay married, he would stay in the closet. I would accept his absences, and we would find our way—together. The boys were not to be told—they were eight and twelve—and neither was anybody else. We had built too much together to abandon our lives. We could adjust—especially me.

What had been Dick's secret, from the time he was eight years old through our courtship, wedding, and fifteen years of marriage, became mine. In twenty-four hours, I went from someone from whom a secret had been kept to a full-fledged secret keeper. The revelation and its aftermath actually brought us closer. The intimacy of a shared secret like ours is hard to equal—except perhaps the intimacy of a real marriage. But I didn't know what that looked like.

Many wives faced with such a revelation take the other route. Furious, hurt, and deceived, they kick their gay husbands out and seek an immediate divorce. Why didn't I have that response? There were so many reasons. I loved the façade we had built of a perfect family, and I couldn't bear to crack it apart. I didn't want to change my life. I had come to believe that I didn't deserve more than he could give me. I was ready to do what it took to preserve the future we both had planned.

Lonely as a child, I always kept my own counsel and took care of myself. I knew how to deal with unfairness and the difficulties strong personalities presented me. I had always put my sorrow and frustrations on the back burner and gotten on with life. So I was ready to compromise. I thought that a sound partnership was the basis of most marriages anyway. Sex doesn't last forever, I thought. Now that we had a shared—very important—secret to keep, our partnership was revitalized. I didn't understand then what it was going to cost me.

For a while, it worked fine. I protected him, and he supported me. When I was commuting to New York, Dick didn't complain, and when the commute became too much of a burden, he agreed to move. It meant giving up a psychoanalytic practice that was full and prestigious, and I appreciated the sacrifice. (It took me years to realize that moving also meant that he would be closer to the man he had fallen in love with soon after he came out to me.) We had a bargain: Dick got two nights out, plus occasional weekends and holidays away. I got my family. He gave me permission to have affairs, though he didn't want to know about them. We pledged our love and loyalty regularly, at home, on vacations, in foreign countries, and on the beach. It looked as if we could survive forever.

We were a team. He took my part every time there was an upset at work, and I edited his scholarly articles about homosexual men. I found an editor for his book and attended all his speeches—about homosexuality—to keep him safely in the closet. There was one especially homophobic analyst whom we considered our enemy. I would always sit behind him at Dick's talks, so I could report precisely how the color of this man's neck would change as he listened to Dick's presentation. Seven shades of red. We had fun. We were together. We shared a secret.

It wasn't hard to keep the secret from our sons. Our habits of kindness and affection didn't change, and the image of a happy home life did not seem to me to be so different from an actual happy home life. We both lied to them about Dick's absences— he was an important psychoanalyst, he had lots of meetings to attend—and they were not suspicious. Teenagers have their own lives and their own secrets to keep.

Then the gay world began to change. Dick's practice was by then wholly made up of homosexual men, and they started getting sick. Nobody knew what it was and how it was contracted. Then his patients began to die. I was stretched out on the bed one evening, hearing the story of the most recent funeral, and I thought I was living a scene in Camus's *The Plague*. I wanted to wake up from the nightmare. I didn't worry about being infected with the disease that soon became known as AIDS, since we hadn't been intimate for a decade. But I hoped that Dick's profound attachment to his lover might keep them both alive. (Neither of them ever became sick.)

This was a lonely time for me, even as solitary as I am. I threw myself into my career. People used to ask me how I had the energy to do all the things I did. "Recycled rage," was my answer. But at the time I thought that my difficult mother was the source of my anger. It never dawned on me to be furious at Dick. I did have one friend in whom I confided. She saved my life. I could phone her when I was so miserable that I was thinking about divorce. She would quote her dad, a retired bartender, who had surely heard it all: "Don't make any sudden moves," she said. I listened.

I was as isolated as a married woman with growing children, lots of friends, and a demanding career could be. I saw my role as the person who was responsible for everybody's feelings— except for my own. I was an emotional meter maid: Are you happy? Good. How's your mood? Fine. The trouble was that I was always on the job. I grew more and more serious. Sometimes my expression was so sad and angry that strangers on the street would look at my face and say, "What's the matter with you, lady?"

At some point, we were sitting in the bedroom and Dick was projecting our future—two old people in matching wheelchairs, being pushed up the street by matching aides. I began to cry. The tears flew from my eyes, not down my cheeks. Something in me was changing.

Then people I was close to began to die: my oldest friend,

my father, and my beloved aunts. I dressed in dark clothing and wasn't much fun. It began to dawn on me that the marriage, which had started in such joy and love and continued as a strong and caring partnership, might not be so good for me in the long run. I went into therapy to see if I could figure out what to do, and it took five years before the choice became clear. I didn't talk much about my marriage with my therapist. Most of our time was spent on figuring out why I was prepared to put up with such a diminished life.

During those years, Dick was having trouble keeping his side of the bargain—to stay in the closet. His gay circle grew, and he found it harder to deny his identity. On the verge of the publication of his first book, we were discussing the questions he might be asked in an interview.

"What if they ask if you're gay?" I said.

"I'll tell the truth."

"But you promised."

"I owe it to my patients," he said.

Something clicked inside me. The bargain would not hold. Dick was having as much trouble in our marriage as I was.

When our youngest son went away to college that August, I lost it. It was too quiet in the house. The home Dick and I had built together was disintegrating. He had the love of his life, even under constraints, and I had the *Goldberg Variations* and a Hebrew grammar book to study. I was so lonely it hurt. I hadn't told my closest friends the secret of our marriage. I hadn't wanted their judgment or their advice. Only one person, my good friend, shared my grief. Dick was away over Labor

Day weekend and I was waiting for him to come home, so I could tell him how bad I was feeling. But when he arrived, before I could speak, he told me that our elder son had come across a clue to the existence of Dick's lover. He was upset and confused by information that made no sense to him. Now was the time to tell him the truth because he would surely pursue this bit of evidence until he discovered the whole story. So Dick asked our son to come home and we sat with him and told him the truth of his father's sexuality. He was shattered. "My whole life has been a lie," he said as he left the house. We didn't hear from him for weeks. I never got the chance to tell Dick that day how painful my life had become. That went straight back to the back burner.

We told our younger son when he came home for Christmas break. He seemed less upset. When his brother invited him to come downtown to his apartment in the Village to talk things over, he refused to go. "I don't want Dad to think I don't love him."

Once the kids knew, I relaxed at home. I was at ease with the secret, at least within the confines of our apartment. So the year passed peacefully, but the loneliness did not abate. By the following June, I knew it was over for me.

I asked Dick for a divorce. The first sentence out of my kind husband's mouth was "I'll do anything I can to help you."

The second comment came from the Freudian psychoanalyst in him. "You're making the worst mistake of your life. You'll never find a better husband."

He said that he wanted to stay married. He found me the

most interesting person he knew, he told me. And he had plenty of time with his lover. It seemed to me that Dick had the best of both worlds. I had the worst.

So as we moved through that summer and into the fall, I told people my secret, and I survived. They didn't blame me, which was such a surprise. I had always blamed myself for not seeing Dick's true nature, and I took full responsibility for the divorce. My friends thought otherwise. Perhaps, I began to think, with this new perspective, Dick could have confided his concerns to me when we were courting. I might still have married him—at that time many people believed that homosexuality could be cured by therapy. But I would have had a choice. And, more important, I would not have blamed myself for my husband's lack of attraction to me.

We celebrated my fiftieth birthday in late summer, the four of us, at a fine restaurant. It was as if nothing would change, even though everything was about to. One of my sons gave me an antique mezuzah that he had picked up on the Lower East Side. It was his way of blessing the new home I would eventually find. It is still on my doorpost decades later.

Today I have come to recognize the pattern of deceit and denial that our family lived. I endured the shock of revelation and the terrible knowledge that my life was based on a lie and would never be the same. I quickly chose to reframe my scenario as one of love and family. That made the deceit palatable to me, and it still does. Dick endured more than forty years of hiding his true self from the people he loved. It diminished his sense of self-worth, to the detriment of his relationships.

He had to be different people in different places, a position nobody would choose. When we were getting divorced, he went to the doctor for a medical checkup because he was so undone by the impending changes in his life. The doctor was amazed: His blood pressure was down, and his pulse no longer raced. His body relaxed at the prospect of his new life, even before his mind did. I was embarking on the unknown, a circumstance not of my choosing but one that was more honest and authentic. I was frightened and had no idea what was in store for me.

Were the choices we made right? That is an unanswerable question. All I can report is that we grew apart, and together, and like weeds at the bottom of a lake, we were deeply rooted in each other's lives.

Over the years in New York, I had run into Jonathan. It happened that he was an editor at Harper & Row, which owned Basic Books. We had the occasional lunch, and I found him as cute as ever, but we were both married. One evening I offered a full-bore apology for jilting him, acknowledging his pain and offering no excuses. He simply nodded and took another sip of wine. I had done what I needed to do, but he was in no mood to forgive.

The fall when Dick and I were getting divorced, I learned that Jonathan's marriage was also breaking up. I forced a mutual friend to tell him my news, and we went on a date or two. We shared our sad stories, and we raised our glasses of good red wine to a better future. Nothing more happened. Then out of the blue he invited me over for a New Year's Eve dinner with some of his friends. I accepted.

My favorite Mozart quintets were playing, and a standing rib roast, my favorite dinner, was in the oven. It felt like home. I stayed late to help him clean up. By the time the dishwasher went on, we had fallen in love again. The rest of that story ends this book.

Part I

THE BOOK OF REVELATIONS

1

THE BIRTH BOMBSHELL

*When a significant secret is revealed, only
the whole truth will restore trust*

Each one of us has our own tailor-made book of Genesis. Who
am I? Where do I come from? What is my destiny? The family stories that answer these questions form the bedrock of our
lives, the basis of our identity. What happens when the revelation of a long-kept secret explodes that story in our faces? It
feels like London in the Blitz. The bombs are falling on our
sense of self, and we have nowhere to hide. We have to begin all
over again. We have to rethink everything, fitting our experiences and all the explanations for who we are into a new story.
We ask ourselves: How could the people I trusted most deceive
me all my life? What else are they hiding?

It is hard to regain trust in parents who never told you that
you were adopted. It takes mental gymnastics to get your head
straight when you learn that your mother is your aunt and your
cousin is your half sister. The world spins when your mother,
who told you she was a widow, informs you that your father is
not as dead as she had indicated.

The people in this chapter have struggled to come to terms

with a most threatening secret: the truth about their parentage. First, they experience the secret for what it is—a profound betrayal. They become suspicious of the motives of the people who lied to them all their lives. Then they harness their anger and energy into searching for the truth. Only knowing the facts will help them create a new identity. For that is another source of anger and anxiety: Their life story has evaporated.

We humans have the unique ability to narrate our experiences—to ourselves. We are constantly processing and shaping the information that comes to our brains from our bodies and our senses. We organize all that input into narratives, which form the foundation of our identity. Some of them are about the past, others are about the present, and we use that same technique to imagine the future. Making these narratives is one of the brain's mechanisms to promote survival. In this way we can massage the chaos of our experience and transform it into our stories. This continuous conversation, much of which is unconscious, allows us to eliminate dangerous options. It helps us imagine survival strategies and even make good gambling decisions.

These narratives are not immutable—they change as our experiences change—but they are fundamental. So when you learn some fact that upsets your founding story, anger, anxiety, and pain are the common reactions. That makes sense. You have to reassemble your identity in a way that accounts for the new information.

In the following pages, you will read about three women who discovered that they weren't who they thought they were.

You will also read about their search for their origins. All three found the truth, eventually. How they succeeded or failed in creating a narrative that allowed them to live with the people who lied to them is at the heart of this chapter.

Naomi, for whom everything that could go wrong did go wrong, suffers not only from the revelation of her origins but also from her parents' inability to respond to her pain in a way she can tolerate. It's bad enough to discover that you have been deceived all your life, but if your questions are met with silence and you can't fathom the reason for the deception, the secret becomes radioactive. In the absence of an explanation from her parents, Naomi created a painful and damaging narrative of her own that warped her life.

The Anonymous Letter

Naomi was writing her dissertation, deeply engaged in the subject and determined to finish it. She was twenty-eight and ready to get on with her career. One day when she came home from the library she found a letter with no return address. She opened it with curiosity. It contained a bombshell: "You don't know me, but I think you should know, I'm a member of your birth mother's family, and you were adopted, and you should know for health reasons." It ended with a promise: "I won't contact you again."

Naomi was shocked. This made no sense. She couldn't be

adopted. Nobody had ever mentioned it, and she had two younger siblings, so her mother was not infertile. Naomi and her husband were outraged. When a bombshell such as this lands, two questions rise to the surface: How could this be true? Why did they lie to me?

Naomi needed answers to both questions, and she needed them right away. Her parents had never been communicative—they were too self-involved, she thought. She knew she needed to be clever in pinning them down. So she called her brother, a lawyer, and together they concocted the perfect question: "How come you never told me I was adopted?" No room for wiggling. Her mother was home, and her father was at the office, so they divided up the calls and each sibling phoned a parent. Both parents gave the same response: "I can't talk now. I have to go."

Their stonewalling was painful for Naomi. Most of us react to shocking news with panic. The adrenaline rush and the anxiety make us restless, and waiting for answers can be agonizing. Think how time slows down when you await pathology results after a biopsy. Every minute seems like a day. This was true for Naomi and her husband. They were desperate for an immediate response and became increasingly furious as the day wore on. They sat by the telephone all day, from two in the afternoon until ten that evening, waiting to hear from her parents.

Finally, when the phone rang, Naomi told her husband to pick it up. She didn't think she could speak to either of them. Her father, a professor and the designated bringer of hard news, spoke.

"How's our girl?"

"Not great."

"I have a class tomorrow, so can we talk on the weekend?"

That was not a satisfactory reply. Naomi's parents lived only an hour's drive away, and if they had responded earlier in the evening they could have driven right over to see Naomi and her husband. Being told to wait until the weekend felt like an insult.

"Too late," her husband said. "You don't have any more chances now."

He hung up. Her parents didn't try to reach Naomi again. They didn't call and say how sorry they were that she was hurt and how much they wanted to explain it all. They let it go. And Naomi let them go. Her response to their delay and subsequent silence was to separate from them. If these people didn't care enough to help her when she needed it, then she wasn't their daughter in any way, and they weren't her family anymore.

They didn't speak for years. She started referring to them as "the Bernsteins." The initial bombshell fractured Naomi's sense of the world, but without help from the people she had known as her parents, she reassembled the pieces in a way that made her story more painful. Their lackadaisical response to the crisis confirmed everything she had long sensed about her place in the family.

"I have a class tomorrow, so can we talk on the weekend?" cast in stone the story of her life as a second-class child. The delay felt familiar. It was how her parents always treated her. Naomi felt that she never came first when she needed their affection and attention. They never had time for her, she thought, and their tepid response to her crisis was just another example of their selfishness and lack of concern. Everything that she had suffered in the family now made excruciating sense to her.

Naomi, as the oldest child with a younger brother and sister, was given heavy responsibilities for the care of her siblings and only glancing attention from her parents. She resented this, but chalked it up to birth order. Even when she went off to college, Naomi felt neglected. During her freshman year her little sister, with whom she did not get along at the time, was having an emotional crisis. Naomi's mother called and told her not to come home for spring vacation. Her presence would irritate her sister. Naomi objected. What was she supposed to do for those ten days, and where was she supposed to go? How could her mother ask this of her? "You give the most to the child who needs it," was her mother's response.

On the day she received the anonymous letter, Naomi needed the "most" from her parents, and they withheld it. So the revelation that she was adopted seemed to explain everything that had ever bothered her. Her serial rejections by her parents and their lack of attention suddenly made sense. She was not their biological child, so she didn't deserve first-class consideration.

Naomi's new story was about the adopted child who never counted as much as the biological children. Other fragments of her life came together to create a new picture. She remembered seeing a family snapshot taken at her college graduation and thinking, "Look at our ears. They are all alike—I must be a member of this family even though it doesn't feel like it." So she had always felt like an outsider. Naomi decided to check her own judgment. "I had one friend left who knew me from high school who knew my family very well." She contacted her and asked, "Did they treat me differently?"

"Yes."

"Birth order?"

"No."

Naomi's revised life story was taking shape. Her parents didn't love her as much as they loved her sister and brother. They didn't care about her feelings. Her personality was different from the rest of the family, and she got on her siblings' nerves. She was adopted—that's why. Why didn't the Bernsteins rush over to her house the day of the letter, and why did they never try to make contact? She was adopted—that's why. This news validated her childhood experiences, but she was still in the dark about the events surrounding her adoption. So in the absence of information from her adoptive parents, she started investigating.

First she went to her university's forensic psych lab to see what they could deduce from the anonymous letter and envelope. It was sent by a woman, probably with secretarial experience (the greeting and the way the letter was folded), who had no special ax to grind. The forensic psychologist said that she should not worry about receiving any further communications from this person, whose identity remains unknown to this day. (The motivation for writing this letter, and the identity of the writer, is still a puzzle. But it changed lives.)

Naomi then plunged into the project of finding her birth parents. Vital records were not digital when Naomi was born, so she got a copy of her birth certificate, with the name of the biological parents blacked out, but a good eye and a bright flashlight solved that. Now she knew who they were. Then Naomi reached out to the networks of people who help adoptees find their birth parents and located hers, as well as the agency through which she was adopted. It was Welcome House, founded by Pearl S. Buck, the Nobel Prize–winning novelist.

Twenty-eight years after she had been taken home by her adoptive parents, Naomi returned to Welcome House with a list of questions. The adoption agency gladly opened their files. Welcome House required that parents tell their child about the adoption when the child is old enough, a progressive policy for that era. Naomi's parents had signed a form promising to tell her she was adopted. They also promised to furnish the agency with a photograph of Naomi, to send along to her birth mother. When the snapshot didn't arrive, Welcome House wrote a letter saying, "Remember you promised . . ." They had kept her father's response in their files. "I'm going to be famous someday," it said, "and we don't want somebody coming and wanting something from us." That letter, and the fact that they did not abide by the policies of Welcome House, confirmed Naomi's opinion of her self-centered parents. But it did not explain the circumstances that led to her adoption.

When she met her birth mother, Naomi discovered a new set of facts. Her birth mother is Japanese, so Naomi is biracial. That explained how she landed at Welcome House, an adoption agency that specialized in mixed-race babies, who were hard to place at the time. Her birth mother had lived in the San Fernando valley when she got pregnant at the age of eighteen. The father would not support them, and nobody would marry her, so she gave her baby up for adoption.

Like many adoptees who find their birth mothers, Naomi felt drawn to this woman. She learned that her birth mother became infertile after Naomi's birth; this kind woman had given away the only child she could ever bear. Naomi felt terrible for her. She had more empathy for the woman who had given her away than for the people who had taken her in and raised her. She reveled in the warmth of this new connection.

Her search for the backstory continued. Naomi was still close to both sets of grandparents, so she went to them to find out what had really happened. Her maternal grandmother said that she had been instrumental in helping Naomi's mother and father find a baby to adopt. Naomi's grandmother was her favorite person. They had always been close, and Naomi believed that her grandmother's love sustained her throughout her childhood. But that was all the information she could wring from that side of the family. Then she went to her paternal grandparents. They were "totally destroyed by my distress." When she called her grandfather, "he would just start weeping." They had been torn apart by having to keep the secret. Naomi was gratified to know that they loved her and felt awful about lying to her all those years, but she still didn't have the story that would enable her to understand her adoptive parents.

Listening to Naomi's tale, I was reminded of the psychologist Harry Harlow and his monkeys. In the late 1950s, Dr. Harlow devised a clever experiment to explore infants' attachment to their mothers. He was working with baby monkeys, whom he separated from their natural mothers. He then created two fake mother monkeys, one made of wire and the other covered in terrycloth. One monkey had a bottle attached to it and the other did not. The baby monkeys preferred the soft monkey, whether or not it gave milk. The baby monkeys showed Harlow and the world that the babies needed more than food to sustain them. They needed softness and cuddling. Just like Naomi. Her adoptive parents, who had raised her in a secure home, educated her, and provided her with all the opportunities they could imagine, were the wire monkeys. They didn't nurture her. Her birth mother, the one who provided her nothing, was now the one she loved.

Naomi and her adoptive parents have stumbled through the decades since the revelation. They began to speak and spend time together again, though the Bernsteins boycotted any occasions to which Naomi's birth mother was invited. At one point Naomi and her adoptive parents went into family therapy, but it didn't work for Naomi. By then she was so sealed into her anger and so sure of her version of the sad story that she could not be helped. She remembers one session in which her mother asked, "What do you want?" Naomi said, "I want you to apologize for hurting me, and then stop. Just stop there." She never got the apology she needed in order to write another version of her life. Still they tried to get together, at least on holidays.

Things almost fell apart one Thanksgiving. Naomi and her

sister never got along. All during the years of hostility, she sided with the parents against Naomi. By now she thought it was time for Naomi to get over it. They were standing in the kitchen, and Naomi was repeating her litany of complaints. The sister got furious. "She said I was trash, trailer trash, and I should be grateful to my parents for adopting me." Her father stood there, silent. Naomi expected him to take her side. She thought he should say, "Don't talk to my daughter that way."

Naomi and her husband gathered their things.

"That's it," she said. "We're out of there."

Naomi and her husband left before the turkey came out of the oven.

The conventional narrative of adoption—we love you and we chose you—never happened for Naomi. Her narrative is: They got me, they raised me, they never loved me as much as they love my siblings, and they don't care to say much more. Naomi is a rejected person, a woman who never quite gets what she needs. She is dissatisfied with the Bernsteins and with herself.

Secrets like the one Naomi discovered need to be followed by the full story, one that explains the motives of the secret keepers and the circumstances surrounding the secret. Answers make all the difference. Honesty begins the cure. An understanding of the secret keepers' motives—both for their actions and for keeping them secret—is needed. Only through understanding the story behind the secret can people find within themselves some empathy for those who misled them. With a bit of understanding—which is at the root of empathy—we may begin to weave a new narrative, one that embraces the truth and plants the seeds of forgiveness. Without the facts, none of this can happen.

Telling is not simple for Keepers who have dedicated much time and energy to the secret. It is painful and humiliating to explain feelings and motives under these circumstances. Even if they believe that they kept the secret and lied to their child for good reasons, they feel guilty. Faced with an angry relative demanding the truth, people tend to pull back. Yet an honest account of the circumstances that led to the secret is often necessary to begin the process of healing. If the Keeper cannot bear to tell the whole story and reverts to silence, the quality of the relationship is put in greater danger.

There are times, however, when the betrayed person is able to find out the whole story without the help of the Keeper. And sometimes the truth is enough.

That was Maria's story. Her father kicked her out of the house when she was seventeen. She had just become engaged to a young man from the wrong side of the tracks, and her parents were outraged. They told her never to come home again. "My daughter is dead," her father shouted as he slammed the front door on her. Thirty years later, she reconnected with him and got the shock of her life. She comes from a family where loyalty and secrecy are entwined. So her search for the truth took her to many new places before it brought her home again.

The Seven Sisters

Maria took her exile literally. She built a good life for herself, without her parents. She broke up with her fiancé and moved to a city far away. Maria didn't even attend her mother's funeral. So when her aunt phoned, imploring her to come home and visit with her eighty-one-year-old father, she was indifferent. "I was not warm and gracious at all."

Maria said only, "Really? Any special reason?"

Still, she accepted her aunt's invitation, and her welcome home after thirty years of estrangement was warmer than she expected. Maria and her father sat next to each other on the couch and talked. Then her father went to the cabinet and brought out the family albums. "We went through old pictures." There's nothing better than old snapshots to evoke loving memories. They laughed and reminisced. Maria drew close. Her father made the first move.

"I'm so sorry for all that happened."

That surprised Maria, and so did the fact that he never received the birthday presents she sent him as a peace offering. Her mother had intercepted them. Perhaps her mother was the culprit in the breakup. It was only after her mother's death that her father sought to reconnect. Looking at the pictures and reminiscing, "we reconciled in the small *r* way," Maria says. Her father leaned back on the couch for a moment.

"I love you," he said. "I can't tell you how much I love you. I couldn't have loved you any more if you were my own daughter."

"His English is not that spectacular," Maria thought. "Maybe he means flesh of my flesh, blood of my blood."

"What exactly do you mean?"

"You didn't know you were adopted?"

Dead silence.

The next day when she brought it up he denied ever having said something so ridiculous.

By now the bloodhound in Maria was on the scent. Her three aunts lived in the house next door. Each aunt had a floor to herself, so Maria went up the stairs, seeking information. It wasn't forthcoming on the first two floors. When she arrived at the top floor she encountered her favorite aunt, the one with a terrific sense of irony.

She said, "My father told the craziest story last night. I asked him where he got me. He said he met a social worker in Chesapeake Bay. Did they deliver babies in marinas?" Maria hoped the joke might entice her aunt into spilling the beans.

"Yeah, yeah," her aunt said, "like Moses in the bulrushes we found you floating down the Chesapeake."

"Well that's cute and funny, but anybody want to tell me?"

"Your father's a senile old man, he doesn't know what he's talking about."

Maria had reached another dead end. Next she went to her favorite cousin. Her cousin shook his head and said, "I am not allowed to speak of that. My mother, on her deathbed, said I must never speak of that."

There's nothing like mentioning a deathbed promise to confirm that there is something to hide. Now Maria had evidence, but she was still frustrated.

"Would somebody at least tell me I am Italian because I'm

so identified with being Italian." Silence. She then got in touch with her childhood friends. One remembered that a schoolmate had lived two doors down from Maria and might know something. She was right, and she phoned Maria.

"Are you sitting down?" she said.

"Yes."

Then she went on.

"Sal and Celia had them two boys, all of a sudden there's this little girl, she's like about four years old, and everybody acted like she'd been there all the time. So we all acted like she'd been there all the time." Maria now knew this much.

"I was dropped, deus ex machina, into the middle of Sal and Celia's house."

She still needed the whole story. Like Naomi, she found social workers who help adoptees locate their birth parents. One night she found a message on her answering machine. It provided the names on her birth certificate. Maria's birth mother was not some stranger but an aunt who had left town years ago. Good. Maria knew where to find her. She was also pleased to know that her birth mother was Italian. Now she wanted to connect with that aunt, who had moved far away from the culture of her sisters.

Maria spoke to her "aunt who turned out to be my mother." It wasn't a pleasant exchange.

"Little girl," she said, "I ain't your mama, your mama lived over there in East Baltimore. Your mama died in Baltimore, and that's the only mama you ever had. And don't you be telling my husband nothing about you being my child, because you ain't my child." Maria did not argue. But her birth mother drove the point home.

"If you do, I've got a gun—and I ain't afraid to use it."

Then Maria got in touch with her half sister, formerly known as her cousin. Things fell into place for them both. Her cousin said, "Now I understand why my mom always said, 'Oh, you should be more like your cousin. She got all A's, she got herself a scholarship, went to college on a scholarship.'" She resented being compared to Maria, and now she didn't want anything to do with her.

Maria tells me this story with a bit of irony in her voice. She understood that her birth mother needed to keep her a secret from her husband. And she saw her half sister, formerly her cousin, being a loyal daughter, which made sense. They didn't need Maria, and Maria didn't need them.

Then Maria went in search of her biological father. The phone message that identified her birth mother also provided a list of men who could be her father and their phone numbers. She set to work phoning them in order. On the eighth call, she spoke to a teenager who said that his father and grandfather bore this name. The age of this boy's grandfather seemed to be right. Maria tells me that she eventually reached a lovely-sounding gentleman. She explained her quest. "Can I ask you some personal questions, like were you in the United States military?"

"Yes, I was."

Oh my God, she thought, don't tell me. "I asked him how old he was, and the math worked perfectly." Then Maria asked the million-dollar question: "Were you stationed by any chance in Annapolis?"

He said, "No ma'am, I'm real sorry, I wasn't." Dead end.

"Thank you so much for your trouble." Maria doesn't know what prompted her, but she asked one more question.

"Would you mind telling me where you were stationed?"

"I was stationed in Fort Meade"—a military base near Baltimore. Then he had a question: "Was your mother nicknamed Bobbie?"

She didn't know anybody named Bobbie.

"I'll tell you what," he said, "I'm going to look in my navy trunk, and if you call me back tomorrow, I'll give you whatever information I have." The next day he told her that he had kept a letter from Bobbie. The return address was Maria's family home.

"I must have cried three rivers of tears, I cried, and cried, and cried, and got on the next plane to meet him." When she arrived, she found her father and his family warm and embracing. They lived a comfortable country life, and on the first night, they took her to a ball game. Maria's half brother was handing out an award to his teenage son, the young man she had first spoken to. Then Maria got the second shock, one that made her think, "I can't be in this family."

Her half brother couldn't read the words on the citation. He was illiterate. His wife nudged her and whispered, "See, Maria, I done told your brother he needs to learn how to read, but he don't think it matters if you can't read. I told him he needs to learn."

For Maria, good grammar is like cleanliness: next to godliness. An avid reader since childhood and an educated woman, Maria recognized that her biological father had raised his family in a thoroughly alien culture. She spent the next few days with them watching exercise and bodybuilding videos and counting the hours until her plane would depart. They were welcoming to her, but as nice as they were, they were not Maria's family. She was appreciative, but she was glad to leave. "I wasn't looking for a new family, but I tried to be responsive to people who were responsive to me because they could have told me to get lost." Just like her birth mother had.

Maria remembers with pride how her parents would sit her on the steps of their brownstone, waiting for the library bookmobile. She'd take a stack of whatever books they handed her, and she'd read them all. This is her family, despite the fact that they did not speak for years, and she belongs to them. So the bombshell of her adoption, which could have further sundered her already tenuous family relationship, actually brought her home.

Maria had discovered a story of the ages: An unmarried woman gets pregnant, and her sister raises the child. Sal and Celia took in their sister's child and raised her as their own. The explanation of the secrecy is also self-evident. They were not about to parade their sister's shame in front of the neighborhood, and they wanted Maria to be a full member of their family, despite the fact that she landed in their house at the age of four.

Her father's apology for the rift in the family was the first step in the reconciliation. Meeting her birth parents confirmed her sense of pride in her upbringing. It helped her to remember those afternoons on the steps of their brownstone, waiting for the bookmobile. She also understood the bonds of loyalty and protectiveness that got her to Sal and Celia's house, and that the whole story was wrapped in family—her family.

Snapshots. Family albums. Reconciliation, even with a small *r*. These elements helped Maria write a new story of her life. If her father had never invited her home, none of this would have taken place. The truth might have come out by mistake, but his love for her turned out to be deeper than she had dreamed.

Maria's story shares many details with Naomi's: secretly adopted into a family, raised by them with contention and conflict, discovering the truth in adulthood, and getting no help in understanding why it all happened. But look at the difference. Naomi never found a comforting narrative, and she got stuck in her pain. Her rage made it harder for her to stay connected with her adoptive family. If we remember Naomi's early sense of being the outsider, her misery fits the pattern of her life. Her parents, by refusing to tell their story, didn't welcome her into the intimacy of their family. Feeling like an outsider from childhood and being denied the story of her adoption, she felt that her family had slammed the door in her face. Secrecy plus silence easily engenders rage. Maria remembers a loving and happy childhood, surrounded by family on all sides. Sure, she fought with her parents as a young adult, but she knew where she came from. So she shrugged off the rejection by her biological mother and was not drawn to her biological father. She knew who she was, and her new story actually strengthened her sense of where she belonged. Same secret. Same truth. Different outcome.

But what happens when the revelation about your origins opens doors to a new reality? That's Annie's story.

Annie's mother, a widow, raised Annie on her own. Her dad had died before she was born. An RAF pilot, he survived World War II, only to die of a heart attack in a Times Square movie theater. It was a tragic ending to a great romance. Annie's mother was pregnant when her husband died, and so she raised her daughter the way so many war widows do: alone, without much help, and with devotion. Annie believed that version of her life story until one Mother's Day when she was in her thirties.

The Mother's Day Surprise

When Annie was a baby, her mother couldn't afford day care, and so she placed Annie in foster care. Her mother would travel to the suburbs by train to visit Annie every Saturday. "We had our routine of going to get a chocolate malt and a pretzel, and then taking a walk." Annie, who was a sunny child and is an exuberant adult, loved her foster family. She made the world work for her by accepting the fact that she had "two mothers and one father."

This wasn't easy for her mother, who once confided to young

Annie that she got depressed "because I would be so happy to see her, and equally happy to see her leave." Annie was finely attuned to her mother's moods, so "the next time that she saw me I had a complete temper tantrum when she left," Annie continued. "We were like a married couple. She lived for me, and I think I grew up feeling a tremendous need to please her and deliver on her expectations." Annie's mother missed only one Saturday. Why? Because she had been hit by a taxicab.

When Annie was old enough to attend public school and after-school programs, her mother brought her home to the city. Annie got scholarships for art classes and music lessons. They visited museums and her mother would sneak her into Carnegie Hall to watch Leonard Bernstein conduct rehearsals of the New York Philharmonic. Their bond of love and mutual respect gave Annie the confidence she needed to grow into the strong and optimistic woman she is. One Mother's Day, when Annie was in her thirties, she decided to come to New York and visit with her mother. Her mom suggested that they climb the stairs to the roof of her building, where they could enjoy the view. On this spring day the air was lovely and mild. They sat together sipping lemonade. Her mother said she had something to tell Annie. "She had exaggerated about my father being dead." Now there's a Mother's Day present for you.

"I was just stunned. It was a combination of fascinated, angry, betrayed, and proud of her"—a common reaction to such a revelation—"because she had lied to me, and I felt all the complexity that goes with being lied to, and being angry about that." Annie shakes her head as she recalls that day on the roof. "It was such a primordial soup of emotions. But at the same time—she had raised me by herself, and figured out how to do it."

Annie, unlike some other bombshell victims, felt gratitude mixed in with her rage. She knew how hard her mother worked to raise her, and she had appreciated her mother's sacrifices and faith in her. Also, unlike Naomi's and Maria's parents, Annie's mother told her the whole story of her birth and the reason why she kept her father's existence secret.

They met doing summer stock and fell in love. She became pregnant, and they were going to marry, but then she had a miscarriage. The high drama of those months, and the mixed feelings about the miscarriage, broke the couple up, and the handsome young man departed for the West Coast. When Annie's mother went to the doctor for a checkup a month after the miscarriage, she got a surprise. She was still pregnant. She had been carrying twins. In the 1940s, long before ultrasound was available, obstetricians were not so good at predicting multiple births. Annie's mother sent the young man a message, telling him about her pregnancy, but she got no response. She hoped he would phone, and when he didn't, she hoped he might turn up at the hospital, and when he didn't, she realized she was alone. Annie's mother and grandmother came up with a solution. Her mother put her boyfriend's name on the birth certificate, and told anyone who asked that he had died in the war. She turned herself into a war widow, a plausible story in those days after World War II.

Now that she knew the truth, Annie was prepared to compose a new story of her life, but she needed to find her father in order to make sense of it all. She had his name and social security number. After some months, she located his driver's license, but those bits of information proved to be dead ends. He had not contributed to social security for decades, and letters sent to the address on the driver's license got no response. That might have deterred Annie from further efforts, but she is a woman of profound determination. She spent the next ten years looking for him. During the course of her search, she became a crack investigative reporter with good contacts. A friend in law enforcement offered to visit the house listed on the driver's license. He knocked on the door, posing as an insurance agent. He said he had a check for Gene Rakoff, but he didn't know if this was the right Gene Rakoff. "And they explained that their daughter lived with my father, on an island in the Caribbean where he ran a diving shop."

Now she knew where he was and what he did, and Annie was torn. She could phone him or not. It took days of indecision, and then she made herself a promise: She wouldn't leave her bedroom until she made the call. A man answered.

"Hi, this is Gene, with whom am I speaking?"

"This is Annie. Annie Rakoff."

"Oh, that's a familiar name! Maybe we're related."

"Yes, your name's on my birth certificate." There was a pause. "Who's your mother?"

"Caroline."

"Ah, Caroline," he said, "I loved her very much, and we were very much in love, and we were going to get married. But I was there when she miscarried."

Annie explained that her mother had been carrying twins, and that she had lost one of the twins when she miscarried, but she was still pregnant—with Annie. Her father said that he never knew about Annie's existence and swore he'd never heard a word about Annie from her mother. Nevertheless, he was thrilled and welcomed her into his life.

"You have great genes, your grandparents are alive. You have two brothers, two sisters. When can I meet you?"

Annie remembers the date she made that phone call, because it was exactly thirteen years later that her father died. She had thirteen years with him, a gift for which she is grateful. Her father was a warm and generous man. Father and daughter met and fell in love. They felt an almost cosmic connection. They finished each other's sentences and laughed at the same jokes. As she got to know her new family, Annie came to understand that her father was a much less responsible parent than her mother had been. He was not an ideal father to his young children, Annie saw, but she was glad to have him in her life now. They romped.

But what about her mother during these years, when Annie was connecting with her dad? "I think she was very hurt, and felt betrayed." Her mother had been forced to tell her secret. She was about to get married, and her future husband was adamant that she tell Annie the truth about her father. He wouldn't marry her unless she told. Annie's mother didn't want to, and to the end of her life regretted her confession. She felt she had been blackmailed into it. She was worried that Annie would turn against her for the lies and that she would fall in love with her father. None of this made her mother happy, Annie says, but she did her best. "She was very grown-up. I know it was painful, but she was in a civilized mode about it, and tolerant." That's how a lady behaves, but Annie recognized her mother's pain beneath the surface.

Robust in her ability to love each of her parents, Annie did not find it easy to live with their contradictory stories. Her mother swore that her father knew about the pregnancy. Her father swore that he didn't know. Holding two conflicting realities in your mind is a special misery. Annie did her best because she loved them both and was not about to choose one parent's story over the other's. But her concern never went away, and so when her mother was dying, Annie tried one last time. She said, "I feel like the one thing I'll never know the truth about is that you say he knew, and he swears he didn't. And I feel like you both have your own reality about it."

"Well, actually I never told *him*," her mother said. He had already left town for parts unknown when she found out that she was still pregnant. She couldn't find him, but she did find his mother. That's who she told about the pregnancy, and his mother kept the secret from her son. That is why the message never got to him. Now it all made sense. Annie called her father with the news.

"My mother told me that she actually never told you."

"I'm so glad she told you the truth."

"Well, I always believed you," Annie said.

"Yeah, but I'm so glad she told you."

The resolution of this last mystery relieved Annie of the need to hold warring realities in her heart. She now could believe both parents and simply relish how much richer her life had become. Her life story is a series of revelations followed by a series of triumphs. Much of her success in coping comes from the positives in her life: a heroic mother, a charming father, and a life with lots of loving support from each of them. And much of it comes from Annie herself. She is an optimistic woman who thinks that her best quality is determination. Her determination got her to her father, kept her with her mother, and enabled her to resolve the paradox of her life story.

Three narratives and three lives that were forever changed. One turned dissatisfaction into misery. The second could have ended in disaster but instead brought a new degree of closeness and acceptance. The third was the longest in coming to resolution, but it ended well.

The differences in the responses began early in the lives of these three women. Naomi never felt included, long before she knew the truth of her adoption. So the sense of exclusion she always experienced was the foundation for her response to her parents' silence. If they had been more forthcoming, perhaps she might have rewritten the story of her origin in a more loving light. Maria began to appreciate her adoptive parents much more profoundly when she could compare them with her biological parents—a mother who wanted nothing to do with her, and a father from a culture that was foreign to her. So her new story had the mythic element of being saved from parents who would have given her a very different life. And Annie, best of all, embedded herself in her new family and discovered her father, a man she thought had been dead since before she was born. By the time her mother died, Annie had found out the whole story, so that she no longer had to juggle two conflicting truths in her heart.

2

A STRANGER AT THE FUNERAL

*A surprise relative appears, and
the family is blown apart*

A death in the family brings up old stories, revives ancient conflicts, and sometimes reveals well-kept secrets. Have you ever been to a funeral where the principals were not on edge? I haven't. Grief has a powerful effect, and mourning makes people vulnerable to feelings they might not have faced for a while. The loss of an important person in our lives forces us to recalibrate old relationships. Meanwhile, we reminisce, we talk about the person who has died, and in those sad moments we try to make one last connection with the person we have lost. Emotions are high, and feelings are tender.

Into this charged situation a stranger may enter. An old friend who had been out of touch for years may feel compelled to attend. A child who had been expelled from the family for ancient misdeeds may be found sitting in the back of the church. An old boyfriend may linger after the ceremony. A former lover appears. People may wonder about such a stranger. But sometimes it is not a stranger—it is a relative whose existence has been kept secret.

Somebody in the company of mourners knows that person. Somebody has been keeping a secret. A big secret. When the truth is revealed under these circumstances, the secret keeper is on the spot. You can't deny the existence of a brother or a sister. He or she is standing there, in the flesh. So what is the Keeper to do? At times like this it seems impossible to come up with an explanation. You don't have the leisure to concoct a story, and you can't easily walk away.

This chapter tells two similar stories. In each of them, a secret sibling appears for the first time at the funeral home. There is no way to deny this person's existence. All you can do is tell the truth—or bend it beyond recognition.

Amy's Shadow Family

Amy's parents divorced when she was seven; her little sister was four. Her father moved away, and Amy's mother took the girls to live with her parents. That was the last Amy saw of her father and his sisters. Amy clung to her mother's family: her grandparents, aunt, uncle, and cousin. They were her family. Her grandparents were gentle people, and formal people. Very New England. Dinners were quiet, life was good, but she never stopped missing her daddy and her wonderful aunts. But that was a background sadness in her busy life.

Amy married, had children, and became a teacher, a very good one. One early-autumn weekend, she had been invited to an educator's conference out of town near her maternal aunt's Cape Cod house. She arrived the afternoon before the conference, and she was alone at the cottage when the phone rang. Amy picked up.

"Who is this?" the voice inquired.

"Well, it's Amy. I'm staying with my aunt and uncle."

There was a silence. Then she heard: "Amy, I'm your aunt, your daddy's sister. Do you remember me?" Amy was shocked.

Of course she remembered her. She had loved this aunt and missed her when they all moved away. Her aunt had called to say that Amy's father was on his deathbed. She wanted her sister-in-law's advice about whether or not to contact Amy and her sister. Amy had picked up the phone and solved her aunt's dilemma. They had not seen each other or spoken in thirty years. Amy's mother was fierce about keeping her girls away from her ex-husband and his family. Amy remembers seeing his car, cruising around the neighborhood, but he never stopped.

When she asked for her daddy, she was told, "Honey, he wasn't a good person, we're better off without him." Since he never made contact with her or her sister, Amy concluded that he didn't love them or care about them anymore. Her narrative of her father and his family was one of disinterest and rejection.

Amy's parents had been high-school sweethearts, but over the years their marriage fell apart. He had trouble keeping a job and they moved from town to town. When Amy's mother discovered that her husband was sleeping around, she left him. Her parents offered to take her and her girls into their home and support them, with two provisos: She was never to see that scoundrel again, and her dating days were over. Amy's mother agreed to both conditions.

When she asked after the aunts, Amy was told, "Honey, they're not like us. Your father's family, they just weren't warm, loving people. They've all moved away, and I don't know where any of them are." Her grandmother and mother emphasized the danger of encountering them. She remembers them warning her, "If my father's family ever located us, they'd probably try to kidnap us."

When Amy grew up and tried to reconnect with her father and his family, her mother threatened to disinherit her. Anyway, she told Amy, that family didn't care about her and her sister, they were not respectable people, and nobody knew where they were. Amy and her sister accepted the story and went on with their lives. So the news of her father's impending death surprised Amy, but it didn't move her. She was more interested in her aunt.

Amy was eager for everything her aunt had to tell. They chatted as if they had never been parted. They caught up on family matters, and Amy got a shock. Her father had a son, who was just a few years younger than Amy's sister.

"I have a brother, I have a brother," she thought. She felt compelled to share the news. She called her sister but couldn't reach her. She called her husband and couldn't find him. She even tried her best friend at work but got sent to voice mail. Amy, alone with the revelation, went to the teacher's conference. "So all day long, it was kind of a zoned-out feeling." When Amy finally got an answer at her sister's home, it was her brother-in-law on the line, who wanted to keep his wife out of this.

"That side of the family hasn't had any contact with you

forever, I don't want to tell her." Eventually Amy convinced him that her sister needed to make her own decision. By that time their father had passed. The sisters decided to attend the funeral. Their husbands agreed to go along for moral support. Eager as they were to be back in touch with their father's family, they were also petrified. On the way to the funeral home, "I was nervous, and I had all of these mixed feelings about I'm finally going to see my father after thirty-something years. My sister was getting cold feet." They stopped to have dinner, "And she was cracking jokes about wanting to go out the back door and trying to find an escape route."

Would they recognize anyone, and would anybody know them? How would they deal with seeing their father again, this time in a coffin? Was his family really so scary?

They entered the funeral parlor. People who were talking in hushed tones saw the sisters. The room grew quiet and the crowd parted. Then the sisters recognized their aunt and uncle. "All my life I thought I'd been abandoned by my father's family, and there they were." These people welcomed Amy and her sister. "They hugged me and said it's so good to see you again after all these years, and do you remember us? I remembered these beautiful aunts who would come and play with me." They held one another and wept.

"I know you want to meet your brother," one of them said. Amy turned toward the doorway.

"My brother came in, and he looked just like my father. He gathered me up and hugged me. And we started crying, and I don't think we let go of each other the rest of the evening."

They talked and talked. He had spent his whole life wanting to know about his sisters and asking when he could meet them, and his father told him basically "the same kind of thing my mom told my sister and me." The irony was not lost on Amy or her brother. The children of this divided family had all been told lies that enforced the separation.

Now it was time to meet their father's wife. Again the crowd parted. Amy's father had run the local movie theater when she was a kid. Sometimes her mother would drop Amy off there after school. She would sit on the lap of the beautiful lady in the booth, who would let Amy hand out tickets to the patrons. Now that woman walked toward her: her father's widow. The woman hesitated. Amy moved forward and hugged her and reminded her how lovely she had been to Amy and her sister and added that she remembered her beautiful blond hair.

"Honey, there were a lot of young blond girls back then." Amy has no hard feelings about her stepmother. "She loved my father, and she was good to him, and I remembered her being kind to me, and as far as I'm concerned, she's my stepmother and I love her. And whatever happened between my mother and father, that was their business." After the funeral, they went back to her stepmother's house. Amy and her sister sat in the living room.

"My brother gave me a book, a photo album that my father had kept. He said that he would find our father out in his workshop behind the house looking at it and weeping. And it was pictures of my sister and me." Then the aunts brought out more albums. "They had this whole scrapbook of newspaper clippings, church bulletins where it would be mentioned that we

57

were singing in the choir, playing handbells in a concert. They had kept up with our whole childhood."

Hidden from view, the relatives followed these girls and loved them from afar. "She and my aunt, and sometimes my grandmother, would sit in the back of the church." They never tried to approach the girls.

Amy's aunt explained: "We didn't know what you had been told, or how you would feel. And we knew from watching you grow up, that your mother and your grandparents on her side were doing an excellent job raising you, so we didn't want to upset your childhood." Sometimes they would drive by the house, just to catch a glimpse of the girls. Sometimes they would see the girls across the village green.

Amy was rocked by these revelations. Then she learned that her aunt worked in the insurance office where their mother had her policy. Her mother visited the office once a month, to pay her premium, and the two women caught up on the news of the family. Amy's mother kept this secret. And her aunts stayed in the shadows. Both sides of this family engaged in an elaborate dance of deception.

"All my life I thought I'd been abandoned by my father's family, and they were there."

Amy was excited to reconnect with the other half of her family, but her feelings were complicated. She felt joy at the reconciliation and regret over the lost years. But she was infuriated with her mother, who had perpetuated the secrets and lies long after the deaths of her own parents. On the drive home, the sisters decided to confront her.

Says Amy, "I told her. And she was stunned."

"Well, honey," her mother said, "if you had called and told me, I would've gone to the funeral with you so you wouldn't have to go by yourself." Amy laughs as she says this. It was absurd. She was thinking, "Right. My father would have come out of the coffin if she had shown up."

Amy witnessed her mother execute one of the classic moves a secret keeper can make. Think of it as an emotional double axel. She denied everything. She erased all the bad words she had said about her ex and his kin. She acted as if there had been harmony between the families all these years. It made Amy crazy to hear her mother deny what she had told the girls. "I don't know what the deal with my mom is. It's like she makes up her own reality that she believes and buys into one hundred percent. And then you can't tell her any different." Instead of facing the truth, Amy's mother changed her story on the spot. Amy found that unforgivable.

Amy kept her mother at a distance over the next year, but this reversal had its benefits. Amy had no compunction about spending lots of time with her father's family. She knew it rankled her mother, but so what. Amy was making up for lost time. She discovered that she is just like them, loud, boisterous, and fun-loving. They enjoy dancing and partying, and even dressing up in costumes—one of her favorite pastimes. When Amy was small, her mother used to ask her in irritation, "Amy, how did you get that way?" Now she knew.

Amy's mother persists in sticking to her revised version of their family story, and it doesn't make her daughters feel any better. "You've just spent thirty years or more of my life telling me you didn't know where these people were, and these weren't good people," and then she did a complete about-face. Amy and her sister both witnessed their mother's lies and threats, though, and that validates the truth for both of them. Their shared knowledge keeps these women sane.

Their mother's ability to rewrite history is not uncommon. We have all seen people change their stories under duress or because of a confrontation. This is part of how we cope. We sometimes feel bad about the mistakes we have made, and regret is not a comfortable emotion. When we are confronted with the secrets and lies we have kept and told, we are on the spot. So we become revisionist historians of our own lives. We see this every day, in newspaper headlines, in political advertisements, and in memoirs. A whole industry of fact-checkers is kept busy chasing down the new pasts people concoct.

For Amy, her mother's revisionist history opened doors to a new family. Amy started celebrating holidays at her cousin's cottage in the White Mountains. Amy's mother didn't appreciate this, but she couldn't object with a straight face. One year, she was invited to come along to Thanksgiving, and she haughtily agreed. The temperature in the cabin plunged when she arrived. Amy's mother played the wronged woman. And then she spotted her ex-husband's son. He looked just like her ex-husband, the last time she had seen him.

She wept and hugged him and said to Amy, "Honey, your father always wanted a son, and before the marriage went so bad, we had talked about having another child. And you know, the way I feel, your half brother could've been my son." Amy's mother latched onto this young man the entire weekend. He later commented, "Amy, I didn't want to be impolite to her. But there were a few times I really had to go pee, and I couldn't get away from her!"

By the time they got home, their mother's improved version of her attitude toward her ex's family was set in stone. She swears she never uttered a bad word about them. She never threatened to disinherit Amy. And even though she was like ice when she first arrived at the cottage, she denies feeling any hostility—ever.

Amy and her sister believe that their mother was afraid that they would prefer her husband's family to her own. That concern turns out to have some merit. She knew that they would never kidnap the girls, but there are many ways of getting children to love you—especially if you are warm and fun and delightful to be around.

Amy and her sister are no longer plagued by their mother's revisionist history, partly because it freed them to get close to their father's family. They understand the constraints under which she lived when they were in their grandparents' house. Now there is no longer any impediment to closeness with his family.

Their mother has no grounds for complaint. The simplest way to deal with revelations is to change your story. That's what Amy's mom did. And, considering what a great family they share, it is fine for their mother to forget the past and get closer to people she had loved before the troubles in her marriage.

Her father's funeral opened up a new world for Amy, and even though she resents her mother for keeping the family secret, she loves her father's relatives. Any regret over past losses shrinks in the face of her present joy.

That rebalancing never happened for Charles. His story also begins at a funeral. Charles was sixty years old when we spoke, and he still struggles to live with the secret that was revealed a quarter of a century ago at his grandfather's funeral.

Charles's Sorrow

Charles grew up in a big family in a small town in the Midwest. It was a hard life, with freezing winters and hot, windy summers. They were churchgoing people, and their Sundays were fully occupied. Lunch at Granddaddy's house finished off the long morning at church. The Bible was read to the family on Sunday afternoon. Charles's father was an elder in the church, and his mother was a leader of the ladies' group. Their religion and its ethics were the foundation of this family's life.

Charles's grandfather was ninety when he passed. He had lived a long and distinguished life. As the patriarch of the family, his home was the central meeting place of all the children and grandkids. Granddaddy and Grandma were the most important people in Charles's life; they supplied the love and support he didn't get from his busy schoolteacher mother and his difficult, authoritarian father. "Grandparents are nurturers. They nurture your spirit." Charles felt like a failure in his home but a success when at his grandparents' house. "When we were children, that was the center of the universe."

Charles often felt that he was a disappointment to his father, who coached Little League, basketball, and other sports. That was not Charles's thing. "I don't have the love of sports that he had. I didn't meet his expectations," he said. "You see, from my point of view, I wasn't worthy."

His father was the kind of man who never admitted that he could be wrong and who believed that anything he said should be taken as truth. The tense relationship between father and son was hard on Charles. Being an only child added to his sense of isolation. His cousins were always over at Granddaddy's house, and he envied the companionship they shared. When things got rough at home, "I would go to my room with my dog and try to heal."

Devastated by the death of his grandfather, Charles was standing next to his mother at the funeral home. They were both admiring the room full of flowers, and she was checking out the cards. This was an extremely hard day for her, because although she was just a daughter-in-law, Charles's mom had been like a daughter to Granddaddy. She was a farm girl who married into the family nearly forty years ago, and they shared a love of growing things. They'd spent hours together in the backyard, gardening and discussing the plants and bushes that would survive their harsh climate, and more time poring over the seed catalogues that littered the house. Over the decades Charles's mom and grandpa grew together like a pair of vines. She was in deep mourning.

The events that changed Charles's life began to unfold in the funeral home. Charles felt a tap on his shoulder. It was his father's brother, Uncle Artie, who said, "Well come on, let's go outside."

"Okay, fine, not a problem."

A woman was on the lawn, waiting to meet Charles. "My uncle was not a womanizer, but he was a Cat Daddy." He loved having a beautiful woman on his arm. Charles assumed she was another of Uncle Artie's lady friends. He was mistaken.

"Charles, I want you to meet your sister."

Charles was stunned. Who was she, and where did she come from? How could she be his father's daughter? It seemed impossible that a man of such probity and high morality could have fathered a child and kept her a secret.

"I can't say I'm really glad to meet you. I'm at a loss for words."

Charles's mind raced. If she was his sister, who else knew about her? Did his mother know? What was his father's role in the deception? Why did his uncle, not his father, introduce her to Charles? If somebody invited her to Granddaddy's funeral, then she was accepted by the family. And if she was recognized as a family member, why hadn't he known about her?

"I'm not here to hurt your mother," the woman replied. That interaction was all that Charles could take. He nodded and hurried back inside. His mother had noticed his absence, but she continued inspecting the wreaths and the cards.

"Who is that woman?" she muttered under her breath.

"One of Artie's ladies," Charles lied.

Throughout the service his mother turned her head to stare at the stranger and kept asking Charles who she was. Charles figured that his mother knew this woman was trouble, but what else did she know? Uncertainty and unanswered questions swirled in his head, as he tried to concentrate on the eulogies and mourn the grandfather he loved so dearly.

After the funeral, Charles confronted his father with Uncle Artie's story about the stranger.

"She's not my daughter." Charles's father was adamant. Charles's mother nodded her agreement.

"This is not my child. I didn't father this child," his father repeated. "As a matter of fact," he added, "the woman had several other boyfriends at the time."

So his father knew all about this. His denials didn't hold up. The very presence of the woman who called herself Charles's sister at Granddaddy's funeral and the fact that Uncle Artie introduced her contradicted his parents. This happened before DNA tests, so there was no way to know for sure. Charles was left to solve an impossible puzzle.

He has a sister. Or so his uncle—and soon his grandmother and aunts—would say.

He doesn't have a sister. Or so his father and mother maintain.

Somebody is lying. Or everybody is lying.

When you learn that you have a relative you never knew about, your universe alters, and you have to rethink all the relationships that are touched by this new family member. But if one part of your family calls this person a relative and the other part calls her a stranger, where do you stand? Charles was experiencing the worst of all possible worlds. He was expected to contend with a giant revelation and juggle two conflicting truths at the same time.

Charles did his best to ferret out the facts. He discovered that his parents were engaged when his possible sister's mother turned up pregnant. His mother had offered to end the engagement and let his father marry this woman. He refused, acknowledging that he had dated this woman, but that was months before he became engaged. Charles's mother accepted that and went ahead with the marriage. For Charles's father to admit that he was the father of this child would have changed the path of his life. Neither of his parents wanted that to happen. So the truth was settled: The child had nothing to do with them.

But across town, another reality played out. Charles's sister attended family gatherings, on the invitation of her grandmother. They just didn't include Charles and his mother on those occasions. They secretly passed her Father's Day gifts on to Charles's father and took snapshots of his girl when she visited. Charles tried to understand his grandmother's decision to accept this girl, but their exchanges were unsatisfactory. "I had many a talk with my grandmother, and I expressed my displeasure." His grandmother's response was both defensive and disturbing: "Well, you don't know if your mother was perfect or not."

What that meant to Charles was that Grandma was prepared to back up her son, whatever he had done. Charles was raised in a family that preached honesty and loyalty. How could his grandmother display such conflicting standards?

"It's not about perfection," Charles protested. "It's about marriage. It's about a bond that those two people have. And if my father chose not to acknowledge this girl to my mother, who are you to accept her?"

That was the end of Charles's closeness with his grandmother, and it broke his heart. The coup de grâce happened when she died. Charles's sister-who-may-not-be-his-sister received her portion of the estate, small though it was. The evidence was clear. His grandparents, and their whole family, accepted this woman as kin, even though they kept up the charade with Charles and his mother.

Charles's mother is supersensitive about this. Some months after his grandmother's funeral, she was leafing through a box filled with snapshots and found a trove of pictures of her husband, his parents, and the alleged daughter. Betrayal! Charles believes that these pictures brought on his mother's heart attack. She survived and has recovered completely. But the fragmentation of Charles's loyalty has not healed. Nor has he come to feel that he shares a common reality with the people he loves the most. Over the years, secretly and with very complicated feelings, Charles got to know his sister. He likes her. They have traded stories and compared lives. Once on the phone, he said to the woman who could or could not be his sister, "This has not been a *Leave It to Beaver* situation here."

"Well," she said, "I always thought that you had your mother and father."

"That was a physical presence," Charles replied, "but an emotional presence wasn't there. I don't know," he continued. "You probably were better off. You don't worry about what you didn't have growing up. Look at what you have now—you have a husband, you have children, and you have grandchildren, and that's something I don't have."

Everybody in Charles's family maintains the reality each prefers. Charles's parents said the girl had nothing to do with them. Charles's grandparents felt comfortable accepting their granddaughter. Charles's father played a double game. He swore one version of the truth to his nuclear family and behaved entirely differently with his extended family.

Unfortunately, these conflicting versions have damaged Charles. He has chosen the explanation that many people adopt when they cannot get to the truth: They blame themselves. Charles has concluded that he is such a nonperson that his family thinks he cannot bear the truth. He's not important enough or strong enough to be trusted with the facts. In this version, his sense of self is compromised. Although he understands that everybody in his family has reasons for holding on to their particular fiction, Charles feels he doesn't matter to any of them. He sees his father as a liar, his mother as a victim, and himself as nothing much at all. His frustration at not being able to get the truth from anybody—except his sister—is an enduring sorrow.

For Charles, believing two conflicting stories is a greater trauma than the secret itself. It leaves him in a special kind of limbo.

Charles compares a secret to a rake. "At the top, it starts narrow, and then it branches out into so many different veins, or fingers, and there's a commonality involved. It still sweeps with the same brush, but it sweeps with different force. It all depends on what it hits. How are people impacted differently, what are the different dynamics involved?" Charles was swept back and forth by his family's conflicting truths.

The events that began at Granddaddy's funeral have changed the lives of the secret keepers, too. After the appearance of his sister, Charles and his father became estranged. His grandmother lost her connection with a favorite grandson. His mother demands Charles's loyal rejection of his sibling. This makes their relationship strained, since Charles's love for his mother is the most sustaining relationship in his life.

Amy and her sister also have to shift from one set of truths to another, but they have each other as a sanity check. The richness of their life with their father's family helped them forgive their mother for her secrets and lies. Charles, whose family increased by the existence of a sister, experienced nothing but loss. He no longer had faith in his parents' veracity and no longer was close with his grandmother. He cannot in good faith connect with his sister so long as his mother is alive, and he has lost confidence in himself. All Charles needed, in order to make the kinds of adjustments we must make in the face of new facts, was the truth. He could have been a happy man with an older sister, whose family he could join. Or he could have stood with his parents in the face of an untrue accusation. Holding two contradictory realities at the same time is damaging. When you are in a perpetual state of uncertainty, you easily come to blame your own character, instead of blaming the people who treasure their truths above your comfort.

3

WHOM CAN YOU TRUST?

*How we stay ignorant when
a spouse is straying*

You wake up in the middle of the night, and you look over to the other side of the bed. You see your sleeping spouse. The duvet moves and a sigh emerges from the pillow, perhaps a little snort. That's the person you married, the person you have built your life with, the person whose love has nurtured you and your children. Look again. Is this a stranger? Are those dreams and sighs about you, or about somebody else? If you can't trust this person sleeping in your bed, whom can you trust?

When you discover that your spouse has been having an affair, the center falls out of your life. Everything you have built, everything you have given, and everything you have shared seems to be for naught. How can I survive, you ask yourself. And what about the children? Who is this person I have been sleeping next to all this time, and who exactly am I? The sense of stability that has been at the bedrock of even a complicated marriage disappears. And the sense of being a lovable person—to your partner and best friend—evaporates. What kind of fool was I? This kind of fool: You are a human being.

One of the central tasks of our brains is to filter information that is coming through our senses into a clear stream. We filter to survive. Think about someone who was blind and sees for the first time. It takes months of training for that person to recognize the colors and the shapes and the objects that were clearly understood by his other senses. The same is true for hearing. It takes a supreme effort for people who were born deaf to distinguish sounds and make sense of them if they have a cochlear implant. If you put hearing aids on, ambient noise is annoying—until your ears adjust to it and filter it out.

It's not that different when your husband or wife begins to change. Little secrets and small lies inject themselves into your reality. Late nights at the office, phone calls taken in the car— we pick up on such things in people we know but aren't married to. But within a marriage, trust may be a filter and denial can be the result. We develop blind spots. We may want to ignore evidence that would require us to face painful facts that might make us change our lives. In the stories you will read in this chapter, you may ask yourself: How could she not get it? What was the matter with him? Our innate ability to filter out unwanted details is one answer.

There is also another answer, known to psychologists as "cognitive dissonance." It's a powerful mechanism that works like this: Once we make a decision, wise or foolish, we like to believe it was a good one; we want to think of ourselves as smart and discerning. If new information contradicts that belief, we experience cognitive dissonance, which is painful. So we unconsciously ignore the new information, shaping our reality instead to fit our sense of who we are.

Plenty of research, mainly by psychologists, shows in detail how we massage our experiences to fit our beliefs. We do it when we choose a car (giving major credence to the positive reviews of the model, ignoring the notion that we might purchase a lemon, even if we have evidence to the contrary). We do it when we watch presidential debates (we love what our candidate has to say and shrug off the comments of his adversary as stupid or senseless). We back ourselves into corners of belief and of denial.

One element in the theory of cognitive dissonance is especially pertinent to marriages, good or bad, true or faithless: the commitment factor. If you work hard for something, you want to keep it and think it is wonderful. This dynamic explains why fraternities command lifetime loyalty. The hazing process itself, which is so unpleasant, is the key to such loyalty. People think: If I survived all that, this must be worth it. I love it, and I'll stick to it. One could think of the planning and expense, the tension and craziness of a wedding as the hazing process for a marriage. That may be extreme, but it makes the point. If a wife or husband senses just a bit that something odd is going on, chances are that she or he will develop just a tiny blind spot, in order to be immune from an attack on the wisdom of the most important choice in life—that of a spouse.

So when the truth dawns it comes as a terrible surprise. It feels as if there were never any clues. Facing the truth of a marriage in which one of the partners has kept a terrible secret can be shattering. It leaves two kinds of residue: anger and truth. The first may dissolve over time. The second can be a building block for a more genuine life.

The difference between the revelations in the previous two chapters and the ones to follow is the importance of the blind spot. Naomi, Maria, and Annie had no reason to doubt their origins before the bombshell event that changed everything. Amy and Charles had no reason to suspect the existence of a sibling. But in the marriages in this chapter we watch a dance of deception and denial. We also learn that the effort to remain oblivious is a costly one, not only for the marriage but for all the people who are involved.

Donna's No-See-Ums

The secret was being kept mostly by me, from me.
And that took a long time to get past.
—Donna

Donna's childhood was laden with secrets. As she was growing up, when scary things happened she was told to keep silent. People who come from a secret-keeping family find it hard to have confidence in their own responses to reality. We need interactions with others to check our own reactions. That's why we discuss movies and books with our friends—to see how our tastes compare. But if you are silenced at home about things that really matter, it is hard to gain faith in your reactions. What can happen, and did happen for Donna, is that you may cede your own feelings to the judgment of another person. This makes it difficult to make good choices and hard to imagine what good choices would even look like. When you hand over that responsibility to a person who doesn't have your best interests at heart, a dangerous shift may occur. You begin to feel as if you made the mistakes yourself. Donna was active in this vicious cycle of lack of confidence and guilt.

When Donna fell for the man she married, she was done for. "This man was the love of my life. From the moment I saw him, that was it." They met in college. "It was a fabulous, visceral thing." She became pregnant and was eager to quit school and marry because all she wanted was to wed this man and hand over all the decisions and responsibilities to him. It was such a relief because her childhood hadn't prepared her to trust her own feelings or capacity to judge.

It took decades for Donna to face who he really was, a man who had multiple affairs during their twenty-year marriage and who shirked most of his marital responsibilities, always maintaining that everything that went wrong was Donna's fault.

The unraveling started early. They were married for eighteen months when Donna got her first clue. "I got a call from a young man saying that my husband was in bed with his girlfriend in New York City and what was I going to do about it." Donna had no answers. At twenty-one, with a baby and no college degree, she couldn't imagine leaving him. She loved him.

They decided to stay together and went into therapy. Things seemed to right themselves—to a point. But Donna couldn't relax. She stayed alert the way somebody does after escaping from a bad situation.

Her worries were a continuous source of arguments. She would accuse him of having an affair and he would deny it, casting her in a bad light for being so suspicious. This is a traditional move of people accused of doing something they don't want to admit—blame the truth seeker for being a snoop (one person I know called such a spouse a Lady Detective). Blaming the suspicious person is a great strategy. You can make that person feel like an idiot or a shrew in order to keep him or her in line. Donna's brilliant PhD husband figured that out. She was a prime candidate for this kind of treatment, and even though she remained suspicious, she also bought his version of herself as a neurotic shrew. When you deny your own instincts in such a situation, the secret keeper gets to set the agenda. And Donna, who had few friends in those years, had no reality check.

When her husband lost his job, they moved to a new city to be near his parents. They both got certified as real estate agents. Donna took to this work with great pleasure. She was a success. In an era when real estate could make you rich, Donna was a star. She made big money and provided the family with a first-rate standard of living. Her husband never found work he liked and after a few bad start-ups, he gave up. Years later, she asked her daughters how their father could square her success with his vision of her as a dimwit. They said their father told them something along the lines of "people who just don't have the intelligence to be able to live the life of the mind, they have to work." He had an explanation for everything.

But Donna was not much fun during these years. When she came home after long and exhausting days running a department of twenty-five agents, she faced a sink full of dirty dishes, a hamper of filthy clothes, and two hungry daughters who needed help with their homework. When she blew up at her husband and daughters, Donna was tagged as a witch. In the outside world, she had daily validation and felt wonderful, but her confidence evaporated at home. Ceding control of her identity to her husband was dangerous for Donna, and it was also bad for her daughters, as she later realized.

Meanwhile, an atmosphere of sexuality suffused their home. Perhaps nudity wasn't so unusual in the 1970s. Still, Donna blames herself for not stopping her husband from showering with their daughters until they were prepubescent and for allowing the girls into their bed far too long. In addition to shrew and dimwit, Donna easily accepted his view that she was a prude. Having been raised in a strict Catholic home, and not trusting her judgment, Donna was again a prisoner of her own lack of confidence.

Deception and denial in a marriage reach past the bedroom. They have an effect on the children, who are confused and angered by the contradictions that surround them. They resent behavior they cannot understand, they mistrust the denials of what are clearly problems, and they tend to believe the person with the answers. So the girls bought their father's line about their mother's stupidity, irritability, and suspicious nature.

Donna had no response to his claims because she thought he might be right. "Then the girls tell me that they'd find this neighbor coming down the stairs when they came home from school, buttoning up her clothes. I had no idea." The daughters couldn't believe that she was that ignorant. What was the matter with their mother? After all, everybody knew.

This is an issue that perplexes parents in bad marriages. If they ignore the facts and decide to proceed as if things were the way they wanted, they can try, but they can't succeed in misleading the children. When the truth emerges, one of the parents gets the blame for being clueless. Donna was an expert at ignoring behavior that brought her pain. She had long ago anesthetized herself. So it is not surprising that the wake-up call that ended her marriage was not an attack on Donna; it was an attack on her eldest daughter.

One night her husband came home in a drunken rage. He turned on his eldest daughter, punched her in the face, and called her a Chink. Donna's husband had been in Vietnam. When he drank, he got mean. That night, when he hurt their daughter, Donna could finally see his behavior for what it was. She started divorce proceedings the next day.

It is hard to imagine this strong-willed, successful woman being such a dolt, but she had been working extra hard to see nothing, nothing at all. Today she has come to terms with his serial affairs. She has accepted the fact of her blindness and the harm it did to her. But she cannot forgive herself for ignoring the atmosphere of sexuality that pervaded the household. It torments Donna. Her daughters deny any sexual abuse, but

Donna knows that she should have been more alert and aware. She should have kicked him out years earlier.

How could she not see?

How could she not know?

How could she not face the reality?

Easily.

Donna had developed elaborate systems of denial. She had multiple blind spots. And every day that she put up with her husband's behavior was another day she invested in the status quo. She accepted his lies, took unfair criticism as correct, and failed to notice behavior that would under other circumstances have raised red flags. It took a physical attack on her daughter to bring Donna to her senses. At that moment her protective instincts erased her blind spots, and she began the long journey of separating from her husband and reconciling with her daughters.

It's no big surprise that Donna came to her senses at the point she did. Her husband's attack might have resonated with some experiences from Donna's childhood, which prepared her for the conditions of her marriage. She had long ago been trained to accept that other people could dictate her most intense emotions. When we are told to keep quiet about a terrifying set of circumstances, it changes the way in which we experience our feelings. We become strangers to ourselves.

Donna's childhood was dominated by her mother's serious emotional problems. This was long before the availability of a variety of antipsychotics and antidepressants. Her parents divorced when Donna and her little sister were young, and then her mother married her psychiatrist, which in those days was not so unusual. When she had a third child, this time with the psychiatrist, Donna's mother suffered from severe postpartum depression. Often when Donna came home from school her mother would be sitting on the couch with the newspaper on her lap. The baby would be somewhere in the house crying, so Donna would rush upstairs to change and feed her. Her mother would stare into the middle distance and smoke cigarettes. Over the months her condition worsened into psychosis.

She became delusional and decided that it was time to end her first two daughters' suffering and deliver them to God. So one afternoon when they were in the kitchen, Donna's mom attacked her girls with a machete. She got to Donna's sister first, and cut her from her chest to her belly. The shock of the blood must have brought her out of her psychosis and stopped her from doing more harm. They rushed the little girl to the hospital, where she was stitched up. The machete had not cut deep, and so she was left with scars but no lasting physical damage. The mother was trucked off to the psych ward. Then Donna's father arrived at the hospital to be with his daughters. Donna remembers the bedside scene as if it were today. She was eleven years old, and her sister was eight. One of the nurses stopped by to suggest some therapy for this stricken family. Perhaps they might want to talk with a social worker, she said. Her father turned to Donna.

"What do you think? I think we can deal with this ourselves, don't you?"

Donna, being the grown-up responsible girl she was, replied, "Of course we can deal with it."

By the time they arrived at her father's house, his message was clear. This incident would never be discussed again. Never. He made her promise, and he made her little sister do the same. For the rest of their lives, her father would brook no discussion of their mother's mental illness or anything to do with the machete.

Even after he remarried, Donna's father simply refused to allow his daughters to bring up their mother's institutionalizations or to criticize her in his presence. His edict of silence was absolute. Many people who grew up in the first decades of the twentieth century believed in keeping a stiff upper lip. Not discussing emotionally laden subjects was a way of life. It is hard to imagine that ethos in our tell-all society, but Donna's father came from an era when silence was considered golden.

After this incident the girls changed schools so that they could be closer to their father, who took over their care. Donna landed in a nicer boarding school, but she was still an outcast because her parents were divorced. She knew she would have been more of an outcast if she revealed her secret. Then she found her first real friend. And this relationship was the first of many that saved her life.

Imagine the scene. It's a dormitory in which ten beds are lined up, five on each wall. Donna's bed is adjacent to her friend's, and they would whisper the stories of their lives after the lights were out. One night, after her friend told her a particularly wild story about her family, Donna opened up. The tale of the machete came out. Donna's friend was horrified. Donna was shocked by her friend's response. She had no idea that what happened in her kitchen was so unusual. Never being able to talk about it with anybody, she assumed that other mothers behaved in similar ways.

She thought that her fear and anger and horror were the problem, not the attack. She felt guilty for the whole episode and wondered why her mother went after her sister first. Donna had long thought that if she had been a better girl, her mother would not have been crazy. That evening in the dorm room, for the first time in her life, she began to realize that her strong feelings had been appropriate. What a relief. The conversation that began more than fifty years ago continues to this day. Donna and her friend lived across the continent from each other when they were raising their children, but now talk on the phone daily and share their troubles and delights.

Once Donna realized that her reactions might not always be wrong, that her feelings might sometimes be legitimate, she began to gain a bit of confidence in herself. But she still couldn't trust her responses to trouble. She became one of those people who must share everything with everybody in order to determine what she should be feeling. Most of us can use the occasional reality check, but a constant need for others to validate your reactions is not useful. It creates dependence, and it doesn't build confidence. And sometimes it is hard to distinguish between people who are genuine friends and people whose opinion is not to be trusted. In her marriage, Donna unwisely ceded the judgment to her husband. It began when she was young and in love, but her dependence on his view of things lasted for decades. She doesn't complain about those years with her husband, but she worries that her daughters may have suffered. So she pays special attention to them and their children. She is clear about what she thinks, and she follows not only her reasoning but also her instincts. Donna has finally freed herself from the specter of that day in the kitchen.

She is a survivor, so with a little help from her friends and a lot of therapy, Donna rebuilt her life. Of course it is still a work in progress. When she found a new passion—painting—she devoted herself to it and to the artistic community where she now lives. She's realistic about her talent, about her ambitions, and content with the life she leads. She's a warm and thoughtful mother and grandmother. She's also intense and sometimes vulnerable. So what. She embraces the world and takes it as it is. She has become a realist.

Donna loves her daughters and her grandchildren. But it's her friends who count the most for her. They aren't as needy as her family. She can't pull any punches with them because they remember all her stories. One of the great benefits of friends, the ones who listen to you carefully, is that their recollections of the important moments in your life are unclouded by the revisions you constantly make. They never forgive the people who harmed you, and they lovingly remind you of your responsibility in the events you regret. Because they love her, they keep Donna honest.

It's funny how you need the support of old friends to help

you face the facts of your life, good and bad. Retreating into a false past or an inauthentic present is so much easier. So Donna, recognizing the importance of her real support system, raises her arms to the sky and says with exuberance, "Thank God for girlfriends!"

Amen.

As a daughter, Donna learned to be silent, and as a wife, she taught herself to see no evil. It was not such a big change for her to deny that her husband was gas-lighting her. She awoke from this slumber when her daughter was attacked. That brought out her protective instincts, ones she had never experienced from her mother.

Childhood offers effective training for adult life. It primes our strengths and our vulnerabilities. This is an important aspect of Janet's story as well.

Janet Learns Too Much

Janet grew up in a family that keeps secrets, lots of them. Her brother and sister were older, and she was the baby in the family. Who knew what, and who told what to whom: These were the channels of information and therefore power in her family. Secrets were the coin of the realm. Everybody played the game: her siblings, parents, aunts and uncles, and even cousins. Thanksgiving dinners were a challenge because it was hard to remember who knew what secrets and who didn't. "I just realized how many ongoing secrets there are in my extended family, parents, siblings, children, nieces, nephews," she says. "It would be good to have a flowchart to keep track of them all. I can almost picture it, the way you do a family tree." Keeping secrets, and keeping track of who knows what, was something of a parlor game in her family. It added to the drama. It added to the energy. You could always have an interesting conversation, chewing over the question of why a relative said this to one person and that to another. This environment gives you the ability to sustain uncertainty and to treasure intimacy. That's how Janet grew up.

This background also helps set the stage for Janet's shocker. It was in the eleventh year of her marriage. One night after a dinner party, her husband was outside talking on his cell phone for a long time. By the time he came in, Janet had already cleared the table and done the dishes. She was in bed when he came upstairs and climbed into bed next to her.

"Who was on the phone?" said Janet.

Then came the thunderbolt.

He told her he had fallen in love with another woman. "And that was the worst moment of my life, the most sick I ever, ever felt, that was the lowest of lows."

Janet experienced a bit of déjà vu. Just a couple of years before this night, her father, the man she had most respected, confessed to an affair he had carried on for nearly two years. His admission was perfectly phrased for a man of his generation: "He basically told me he had good news and bad news. The bad news was that he had had an affair for two years, and the good news was, it was over." Janet could hear no good news in that. She felt that she had been betrayed, along with her mother.

The Keeper in Chief of family secrets is her mother, now in her mid-eighties. She never discussed her feelings about the affair with her children, but "she told my brother that during the time when my father was actively having an affair, she wanted to drive her car into a brick wall." Now the two men Janet had trusted most in the world had fallen from their pedestals. The day after her husband's revelation, she went home to her parents. "I thought it was the perfect moment for my mother to confide in me, commiserate with me, empathize. I was hoping that it would be the perfect lead-in for us to talk, woman to woman, about how much it hurt." She got no response from her mother. Then she had it out with her father. "I didn't hold back in letting him know just how much it hurt to be the scorned woman." Again, he made no connection between his past and her present. This was not helpful, either. She was on her own.

Janet wasn't about to cede her marriage to another woman, so she insisted that they go into therapy, which her husband agreed to. After a year of intensive work, things settled down. She was vigilant with her husband, accompanying him on his travels and watching things carefully. Over time she thought the marriage was saved. "I was so proud of myself for working so hard on it." She patted herself on the back, saying, "Wow, we really did this, and we're really in love!" It was a good time. "I thought that we were home free, and I was so excited to be facing the rest of our lives together with an intact family." Janet used to tell her kids, "So-and-so got divorced, but you guys are lucky, because your mommy and daddy picked the exact right people for them." Like Donna, Janet was expecting a big return on her investment in couples therapy. But then clues started registering again in Janet's consciousness.

In the summer of 2002, Janet noticed a series of suspicious e-mails, and she started to investigate. By the end of that summer, she was certain he was at it again. They had planned an autumn trip to the mountains for their fifteenth anniversary and Janet considered canceling it. "I decided to just go and be miserable in the country rather than be miserable at home alone with him." That night at the resort it all came out. "He described to me every woman that he had been seeing." There had been many in those four years. The revelations continued. "He also told me which hotels he used. He told me what birth control they used, or didn't use." He told her details that no person in their right mind would tell their spouse. Unless he wanted to leave the marriage, that is, which is what happened. It may be that her husband unveiled his secret life in such detail in order to force Janet to face the reality she had ignored for so long.

This chronicle of betrayal seems cruel in the extreme. It was extreme. But it may be that Janet's husband, having left her little crumbs of his behavior for years, couldn't stand it any longer. He needed to shock her out of her denial. And shocked she was. Sometimes a gradual recognition of reality feels preferable to the shock Janet's husband administered. But the series of revelations was so strong and brutal that she was left with no alternative but to face the reality and get rid of him. These years began in deception and ended in brutality, but end they did. Now a clean break would allow Janet to begin the healing.

After the divorce, which happened quickly, Janet's ex dropped his most recent girlfriend and married another woman. Janet is over him and has come to terms with her former husband's personality. She sees him for who he is, and she would not want him back. Her perspective is historical. "I think part of it started with 9/11. We both had different attitudes. My attitude was: What a horrible thing, we need to keep our loved ones close, and hug them and love them and cherish our families and be glad we're alive. His thing was: I haven't lived enough. I haven't sowed enough oats."

By now the oats have been sown and the children have grown up, and Janet has a life that is more grounded in reality. Her patience for secrets and lies has diminished. And she tries to keep her blind spots to a minimum. Reality may make for a less romantic life, but it does offer a sense of security she never had with her husband.

Denis, who got a terrible shock one afternoon, says, "It was to me the darkest hour of my life." But like so many people whose lives are torn apart when they discover the truth about a spouse's affair, Denis has been able to make a new life, over time, and a better one.

Denis's Boomerang Life

Denis sailed through his life and marriage, never dreaming of what was happening at home when he was away. A graduate of an Ivy League university and a successful executive at a Fortune 500 company, Denis thought that life was beautiful. He and his wife and seven children lived in a pleasant suburb, and he brought in such a good income that his wife didn't have to work. They had been high-school sweethearts and he had risen to the top of his profession. He knew he was the right man for her.

To help out with their brood of seven kids (the youngest a pair of twins), Denis's wife hired a high-school student to come over in the afternoons and be with the children—mainly the three boys. "He played golf with them, he was a pretty good athlete so they liked having somebody that's fun to be around." The daughters didn't have much time for Bob, and they were the first to sense that something wasn't right.

"Bob and Mom sit kind of close together when they're watching TV," they complained to their father. Denis shrugged this off. How could a high-school kid compete with him for his wife's affections? "I just didn't see it."

Even Denis's parents, who visited regularly, were disturbed. His father once asked, "What's this kid hanging around here for? Doesn't he have friends his own age?" Denis's mother had her own suspicions. "I see them talking to each other real close and whispering," she complained. Eventually Denis's parents stopped coming to visit.

Still, Denis was oblivious. There was no possibility that the babysitter, a high-school kid who was nice but not interesting, could be attractive to his wife. "It was so far-fetched in my mind, I never even really paid attention or put together these comments that my parents and my own daughters made."

Their marriage seemed fine, and there were no big fights. Denis's week was spent at meetings around the globe, and he was exhausted when he came home, but as he saw it, they had a good relationship and a good sex life. You don't know what you don't see until you are forced to see it.

Denis may have been misguided, and he may have been naïve, but eventually the dropped clues got the best of his denial. "She was telling me she was one place and was in another, and then I followed her a little bit." That's how the discovery started. "I found she was secretly meeting the kid. And then I went over to his dad's apartment, and I confronted his dad. I went into Bob's room, and he had pictures of my wife all over."

This was the moment Denis describes as the worst of his life. Not only was he furious, he was humiliated by the fact that she was having an affair with a boy only five years older than their eldest daughter. How could she have fallen in love with him?

"What a dope I am," Denis thought. "Everybody saw it except me. And I'm the guy who's in bed with her at night."

Denis's life crashed around him. He had built it with his wife and looked forward to their future. He didn't love traveling every week, but his success was the route to a secure old age, which he planned to spend with his wife, the girl he had taken to the high-school prom. Everything he had worked for, planned for, and hoped for was over.

Divorce proceedings began. It was Denis's good fortune that his company was part of a corporate merger during this period and in the transition he was let go—with a golden umbrella. He hates the fact that his wife got part of that money, but his share allowed him to go back to school for a teaching degree instead of trying to get back on the executive treadmill. Denis got custody of all seven kids, who wanted to have nothing to do with their mother and her boyfriend. It was the end of a terrible chapter and the beginning of a better one. The truth gave Denis a second chance.

Denis could no longer stand secrets. He no longer wanted to play the fool or to fool anybody in his family with the small falsehoods of everyday life. His misery faded as honesty took the place of secrets. He knew that to embrace truth, he had to start with himself. It was the first building block of his new life. "I made my own personal vow, not just to have no secrets but to never not tell the truth." This is what he told his kids: "Look, I'll never lie to you. I will not. I may refrain from saying something, but what comes out of my mouth is the truth."

Over the next twelve years, Denis began to relax. "I've always said the softest pillow is a clear conscience, and I sleep like a baby every night." Denis was able to stop traveling and spend seven days a week with his kids, getting to know them better and being present not only for their games and performances but also for their troubles and pain. He waited until the children were out of the house to remarry, and he is happy with his new wife.

The decade between divorce and remarriage gave him something he never expected. "In my forties I did everything that I wanted to do," including dating lots of women, before he fell in love. He coaches high-school sports and loves it, especially the girl's varsity basketball team.

What about the first wife? She married the babysitter and has a child with him. Is Denis still angry? Sure, but he thinks she's going to be in for it, eventually. "Do I think my ex-wife's gonna get hit by a bus sometime, and that's karma? No." Denis is more of a realist than that. He knows how to count. "Guess what? She's fifty, and he's thirty, so let's do some math here. And she's got a seven-year-old daughter, so when she's sixty, she has a teenager." Denis concludes the arithmetic exercise. "And when she's sixty, he's forty."

Denis will never get over the shock of his wife's affair and the destruction of his first life. But he understands more about her relationship with the babysitter: For her, being the center of someone else's life is magic. She loved the fact that there was nobody else in his world but her. She and Denis did not have that kind of relationship, and he either didn't know what she needed or didn't want to provide it for her. When he faced that truth about their marriage, Denis began to understand her odd choice. His empathy allowed him to divest himself of some anger and hurt.

Denis has found a new life, due in part to his resolve and in part to good luck and timing. Building a new life isn't fun, but many people do it. They can count themselves fortunate if they take Denis's point of view: "Look, if that's the most horrible thing I ever have to go through, then I've lived a charmed life."

The three people in this chapter all worked double shifts to ignore the reality of their marriages. Denial was as much a part of their relationships as their partners' adultery. When the truth cannot be denied, but people decide to continue as if nothing has changed, what changes is who they are and how they survive in the world. From Donna, Janet, and Denis we learn that keeping secrets from ourselves has its own high price.

4

WE STAYED MARRIED FOR THE CHILDREN

When we deceive others,
we diminish ourselves

Those of us who have lived long enough understand that it is a mistake to try to make judgments about other people's marriages. We know how hard it is to fathom our own marriages, much less other people's. Couples who seem to be at odds stay married forever, and the lovebirds next door may be discussing the terms of their divorce. What does she see in that lout? How can he bear her carping? The answer comes in two parts: It's none of your business, and the reasons why they're together would probably surprise you.

Marriage is the bedrock of the family, and families have been the survival mechanism of humanity from the beginning of time. For much of that time, there were no easy alternatives to staying married. Religion and the state made divorce almost impossible. Many couples were too poor to part. One partner scratched out a living, and the other raised the children. Couples worked together to keep the farm going, or slept above the store. When survival is at issue, compromise is one answer and misery is another. When compromise is no longer possible, the choices seem to narrow. The decision to stay married in a difficult situation is not easy, but neither is the alternative.

One of the most common reasons for staying together in a bad marriage in modern times is because of the children. It's a fine reason. It sounds good; and noble sacrifice is written all over it. And the costs of staying in an unhappy marriage for the sake of the children may not be apparent at the outset. It's not just the conflict, the frustration, and the possibility of betrayal we need to consider. There is also a substantial price to pay for enduring and providing everyday doses of deception and denial, as we've seen with Donna, Janet, and Denis. These have a powerful impact on self-image and confidence. What may start as a simple set of secrets can spread through a person's character like a cancer, one that is not easy to remove.

It takes a lot of effort and tremendous energy to keep up appearances, especially at home, and to deal with differences—especially in front of the kids. The shared secret of an unhappy marriage means that the partners have adopted a stance that values stability over honesty. Some couples make an effort to conceal their anger and sadness. Keeping a secret like this demands habitual denial, which gradually may morph into self-deception. While it may seem best for the children, and some experts do suggest staying married for their sake if the marriage is low in conflict, the side effects include the decline of intimacy, the attenuation of trust, and the diminution of the self. This change in the relationship may be obvious in the home or it may remain hidden behind the bedroom door. Either way, it alters the atmosphere in which the children grow up.

Unhappy marriages are always fertile ground for secrets. But couples who explicitly stay married for the sake of the children go a step further, working consciously to create a new reality for themselves and their spouses. Think of this as a necessary delusion. And it takes energy. If the job description is to keep up appearances, in the home and outside of it, adjustments must be made. You must hide the painful facts of your differences and act as if nothing is wrong. You must push your conflicts underground. The charade is made possible by the fact that we are all born with the ability to fool ourselves and to compartmentalize different aspects of our existence. We have the capacity to put pain and sorrow on a back burner for a long time—if we so choose.

Donald's Alternate Universe
Keeping it secret, and leaving without leaving—it
was all wrong.
—Donald

Donald and his wife fell in love their freshman year of college. She became pregnant, and they married. She quit school to support him for the next three years, babysitting in addition to raising the first two of their three daughters. This was a sacrifice for Donald's wife. She postponed her education and was perpetually exhausted. After he graduated, Donald got good jobs and became a successful executive, thanks both to his wife's sacrifices and to his energy and ambition. His wife, having supported them through those college years, stayed home to raise the girls, and Donald heartily approved. But she never seemed to get over the years when she'd had to earn the money and count her pennies to provide for them. This kind of resentment is hard to erase, when the person you supported becomes successful—perhaps especially so. Her anxiety about money translated into active resistance to spending any money on their daughters.

Over time, the relationship deteriorated. Donald traveled during the week, and when he returned they didn't have much to talk about. She was critical when she heard stories about his work, and her days at home were of no interest to either of them.

Because his wife was fearful about spending money, she refused to pay for the things their daughters wanted and Donald thought they deserved: lessons, bikes, trips, and the like. They all thought she was just cheap. Donald would listen to the girls' complaints after their mother had refused them—and then give them exactly what they wanted. Eventually, because this caused so many arguments, Donald established a secret ministry of generosity, shutting his wife out of the conversation.

If one of the girls wanted voice lessons, she would go directly to her father, who would agree, arrange the whole thing, pay for it, and then inform his wife, who felt constantly and thoroughly undermined by this behavior. The conspiracy between father and daughters was not good for the marriage. Presented with a fait accompli, Donald's wife would explode in rage, but she had no recourse: the daughter had already been signed up, the gift was already bought, or the bill was already paid. When Donald was out of town, his wife would blame the girls, accusing them of bankrupting the family. These accusations were duly reported to Donald when he came home.

Donald's wife had sacrificed her education and future to support him through college, an essential element in his success. Now she was stuck at home with no authority and little energy for activities that might have brought her more satisfaction. She felt Donald didn't respect her enough to abide by her decisions about money, and he did not show gratitude for her sacrifice by honoring her wishes. Donald had diminished her power over the girls, whom she raised all week while he was on the road. He was spoiling them behind her back and undermining her. No wonder she was full of rage. When Donald came home, the girls greeted him with horror stories about their mother and then made more demands. So new secret pacts were sealed.

Meanwhile, Donald was traveling and spending his generous expense account when he was away. But now the secrecy and silence were having an effect on him. He was drinking heavily on the road and meeting women. Late nights at bars and sexual affairs became his way of life. "I basically gave up on the marriage. I planned on staying until my youngest daughter graduated from high school." The affairs continued, and while Donald felt bad, he mitigated the guilt by thinking of what he was doing for his daughters. "I considered myself throughout the marriage as the one who stood between them and their mother's moods. She'd get so wound up that she needed to lash out. And when she started attacking them, I stepped in between." Since he was meeting his obligations to them, and since his wife was angry and resentful no matter what he did, an affair or two wasn't such a big deal, he reasoned.

Keeping little secrets like arranging for dance lessons had metastasized into a whole world in which Donald did exactly what he wanted, when he wanted, including plenty of one-night stands. But he didn't enjoy it. "I didn't do them because they're fun—they're not. I did them because I was in control and nobody knew what was going on." Donald is honest about what he felt and clear about his behavior. "It led to me being able to justify awful secrets. And I was able to justify my bad behavior because of hers. Which is not right; there's no justification at all. It's an excuse. You know, the human mind is great at justification."

Donald is right. As we've seen, our discomfort with cognitive dissonance enables us to rationalize our decisions, right or wrong. Donald knew full well what he was doing, and on some level he felt bad. But he quickly rationalized his actions: He had to care for his girls.

The status quo altered as Donald approached his fortieth birthday. The girls were grown, and Donald had fallen in love. He decided to divorce his wife and build a life with his new lady—and the new baby who was on the way. Donald knew that he had treated his wife badly, but he believed that he had done right by his daughters. He planned to take good financial care of his wife in the divorce. Donald was not surprised at her outrage, but he was shocked when his daughters sided with their mother. He had no idea of the depth of their love for her and their loyalty. She was always there when they needed her, and her presence and love counted more to them than all the lessons and presents their father could buy.

Donald's decision to divorce burst his bubble of self-deceit, which had served him so well over the years. He had to face what the girls were thinking and feeling. They hated the new reality in which their father was no longer Santa Claus and their mother was no longer Scrooge. Like so many children of divorce, they wanted things to stay the same. And they properly blamed him for betraying their mother. They were at a loss, ignorant of what their father was feeling. Today Donald is working to reconnect with his daughters, but he continues to be stunned by the force of their anger.

Donald has learned a lot about himself from all this. Recognizing the toll that secrecy played in his first marriage, Donald understood that in order to achieve an authentic relationship and intimacy with his new wife he had to unlearn his habits. Honesty was essential for the relationship he craved, and he realized that it was the only way he could become a full partner in the marriage. He started with his bank accounts. Donald made them all joint accounts with his new wife. For him the symbolism was immense. No more secret expenditures, no more sneaking around, no more clandestine drinks and dinners—he was a new man about money. He loved it when she began to pay the bills and watch their expenses. Credit cards were next, and another opportunity to cheat disappeared. Donald craved transparency, which is an essential element for closeness and intimacy. But there was more to come.

Passwords: He shared them with his new wife. She started running his Facebook page, and he was thrilled. Cell phones: Another escape route for Donald that he turned over to his wife. She has lists of all the numbers he calls and all his incoming calls, too. A woman who is adept at the computer, she can keep all the information they need about his life—and he has no secrets.

This decision to come clean and stay clean has been a work in progress. Just recently, he was on the phone with his first wife when his new wife walked into the room.

"Who is it?" she motioned.

"Nobody important," he mouthed.

After he got off the phone, Donald realized what he had done, so he admitted that he had been talking to his first wife. This didn't matter to her, but it meant a lot to him. Donald is aware of every step he needs to take to open up his life and share it with the woman he loves. He has also stopped drinking heavily. He is so much happier now that he is not keeping secrets. "It's like this slow unwinding of a spring. The more I've done, the more I've been able to relax."

Donald didn't like being a secret keeper, even while he was justifying his behavior. "I grew up in Wyoming, and there were a couple of basic, core things that I was taught. One of them was honesty." Now he can cleave to that value. His eldest daughter, when she visited with him, commented, "You're just much happier now. And much, much nicer to be around." Donald finds it easier to be with himself now that he has changed his situation and changed his ways. It's not fun to be a liar and a secret keeper. Tension and distance are the side effects of keeping secrets, and Donald told himself it was worthwhile to live that way for his daughters. But he is happy to have straightened out his life and his soul.

Margo also regrets lost years spent turning herself inside out in order to stay married—all for her children. She was on the receiving end of her husband's secrets and lies, but found she could only sustain the reality of her life by lying to herself, too.

Margo, the Pretzel

Margo was married for twenty-three years. Five of them were good, and the rest were not. Listening to her story, it seems clear that her husband fell out of love with her about the time their first child was a toddler. He just didn't have the emotional energy for children. His work took him out of town for weeks at a time, which became months at a time. When he was home, he was almost as absent as when he was away. Short-tempered and critical of Margo, her husband left plenty of clues about his life outside the marriage, but she was intentionally credulous. For example, when he returned from a long trip and was unpacking, an earring of unknown origin fell from his suitcase.

"Whose is this?" Margo asked.

"Isn't it yours?"

No, it didn't belong to Margo. It was something she would never wear. But she didn't have the heart to follow up. She dropped the subject.

Things had started out so well. They agreed about politics and about ethics, they were an ambitious couple who worked hard to make names for themselves, and they both wanted to have a family. Margo was proud but worried as her programmer husband became a software mogul, with all the attendant perks. "I would say to him, 'Let's not get used to this, it scares me.'" She had reason to worry. Soon he seemed distracted, even when he was playing with their delightful little girl, and especially when they were alone together. Fun dinners with friends were great—but when they got into the car, silence.

What bothered Margo most was his lack of interest in their daughter. It was the first major dispute between them. He left the house early and came home late, so he often didn't see his child for days. When he left for work, she would cry, "Daddy, don't go." This statement likely reverberates with most parents. It's part of raising children. But Margo's husband didn't like the conflict. So he would phone to say, "We're having dinner with so-and-so. I'll pick you up around the corner, I don't want to deal with her now." Margo always checks with the experts, so she called the pediatrician, who said that even if it's painful, he should come home and see his child. But her husband refused. Over the next few years his mood darkened, and he started to bark at Margo and the children (now there were two).

Margo began to mold her behavior and the children's to his needs. "We're very well behaved now because we don't want to get him upset."

In her effort to be the good wife, this witty and prominent art dealer gave up her work to concentrate on the children. She stopped shaving her legs, and she stopped thinking of herself as smart and funny. She couldn't tell anybody how miserable she was. Her parents had been married for half a century, and her younger sisters were building their families. When friends seemed so happy with each other, Margo watched them with envy. Two kitchen scenes sum up her discontent. "I was in the kitchen getting ready to serve something, and a plate had fallen and crashed, first on my head and then on the floor."

Their friend called in to the kitchen, "Are you okay?"

Before she could answer, her husband, who was in another room and couldn't see her, replied, "She's fine."

"I'm not fine," Margo thought.

She remembers going to another friend's house for brunch, and her friend's husband asked, "Honey, can I make you a cup of coffee?"

"Wow," Margo thought. "Is that how real people talk?"

The sad moments piled up. But Margo was fixated on her goal: two beautiful children and a successful, happy marriage. She went back to work, and that felt good. So did the fact that she was pregnant again. Then, at a meeting to discuss an exciting new artist, Margo felt something. She was losing the baby. She had a miscarriage in the gallery bathroom. She felt awful. It was especially hard for her because she'd had trouble carrying their first child, and she desperately wanted this third one. So she called her husband, who was at a meeting in Paris. She told him the sad news and asked, "Could you please come home?"

"I'm in the middle of a conference."

They eventually had another child.

Also devastating to Margo was a moment soon after 9/11. She found herself in a building where they had discovered anthrax and phoned to tell her husband.

"I'm on the other line," he said.

When Margo and her husband sought counseling, their first therapist commented, "The two of you are like metal grating against metal." They ignored that. The second therapist told Margo that if she wanted to stay married, she would have to lower her expectations of her husband's behavior and of what happiness meant. Realistic advice, perhaps, but hard to take. The standoff in their marriage went on for years. Margo found it hard to keep her spirits up, and she confided her misery to a friend.

"Would you lay down your life for the children?" this friend asked.

"Of course."

"Then stay in the marriage for them."

She did. Why did her husband stay? By this time he was living away from home most of the time and enjoying the company of other women. The sex appeal of a mogul is hard to equal. He had things just the way he wanted, and when Margo got suspicious and questioned him, he denied everything. He stayed away more and more. If he were expected home at the end of a week, he'd call on Friday to say that a meeting was being held over until Monday. Margo stopped minding his absence. At least there was no friction, and she had become accustomed to being both father and mother to the children.

Margo opted for secrets and lies, lying to the world for her husband, taking his phone calls in another room so the children wouldn't hear the arguments, making up for his absence in every way she could think of. She wanted her children to grow up in an intact family, and with the help of her parents and sisters (to whom she never confessed her troubles) and some friends (who knew the truth) she did the job, although she had to work overtime.

What was it like for Margo during those years? She had become an expert at ignoring the truth, so she didn't think, "Wow, that was good, they still don't know."

She was not proud of herself, so she didn't think, "I held it together today."

Margo was spent, and sad, and her last thought before falling asleep was, "How am I going to manage tomorrow?"

The children didn't know what was actually going on, or why, but they noticed the fights and the tense atmosphere. When her youngest was nine, he said, "Daddy and Mommy, we have to have an intervention for your marriage," and Daddy said, "I'm too tired, let's do it later."

Margo noticed the older kids bickering just like she and her husband did. It made her anxious. Things finally came to a head the week of their eldest daughter's sweet sixteen party. Her husband arrived just as the party was beginning, but he took Margo aside for a moment to tell her that he wanted a divorce. The celebration went on as planned, with loving toasts from both parents. Her husband was not prepared to actually leave yet, but the issue was finally on the table. When Margo's friends encountered him having a romantic dinner with another woman, he told them that, sure, there were problems in their marriage, but Margo knew all about it. In this way he was able to protect himself. That strategy left Margo thoroughly vulnerable.

Why did Margo put up with this? Fear, loss of prestige, loss of the illusion of a good life—these were all part of it. How could she bear to put up with it for so long? Margo experienced something like Stockholm syndrome—she identified with her captor. She internalized his criticisms of her housekeeping, her looks, and her talent, so she began to believe that she was an unattractive slob with mediocre gifts. These accusations were false, which Margo now acknowledges, but in order to make herself believe that everything was okay, she needed to accept the negative view of herself. A kind of perverse logic was at work. If she saw herself as undeserving of her husband's love and respect, then his behavior made sense. This reversal of the facts made it possible for Margo to survive.

Think of Margo's life as an algebraic equation. First she had to solve the part on the right of the equal sign: *I am going to be content with my life, because this is what I want and it is best for the children.* But then she had to adjust the part on the left. And her way to solve it, which is far from uncommon, was to minimize herself: *I am not so smart, I'm not attractive, I can't meet his expectations, and I don't deserve his love.* Now the equation was solved: Unacceptable Margo gets what she deserves.

Eventually they decided to divorce and told the children. Even though their father was rarely home, was nasty to their mother in their presence, and seemed angry and irritable, they were shocked and miserable. The two older children started to cry and scream. Their memories of the good years when they were small and spent time together as a family trumped the reality they had lived for a decade. The youngest child, playing his video game in the hotel room where the announcement was made, didn't look up. By the time he was born, his father had all but moved out of the house and on to his new life. This son knew that very little in his life would change.

Everybody has a new life now, years after the divorce. Margo's former husband has a new love. He is a reformed man—at least as far as his new family is concerned. He is an attentive father to his girlfriend's three children: He attends their games and performances. He goes to their parent-teacher conferences. He never did any of that for his kids. Like Donald, he is reforming— with his second family. This may show that he regretted his behavior with Margo and their children. But Margo's children have not benefited in the least from their father's supposed change of heart. And they notice the difference. It doesn't make them feel good.

For years after the divorce, Margo, to her surprise, was the major target of the kids' demands. They would tell her that she was the responsible parent, the one who took care of them, and so she had to meet all their needs. They'd given up on their father—all the more reason to rely on her.

To protect her children, Margo still kept secrets. She kept the details of her unhappy marriage from them. She believed that information was dangerous. Only the eldest knew that their father had been serially unfaithful over decades. None of them knew that he'd refused to come home when Margo miscarried—they may not even know she miscarried. The anthrax story never came up.

Kids often beat up on the parent they are closest to—that's the parent they can trust. Margo's children did not want to antagonize their father or to lose any more of his time and affection. It was not worth the risk. Margo sighed and accepted the burden of being the parent who was patient, accessible, and always blamed. Her acquiescence was certainly due to a deep commitment to her children. But the situation was also fueled by her habit of keeping her feelings to herself and pretending that things were all right. The children's attitude grew out of her decision to keep them in the dark: She hid her unhappiness, glossed over a reality they all experienced, and did not respond in kind to their angry father.

Margo was genuinely glad to be free of her husband, but she didn't enjoy being the de facto single parent of teenagers. Still, she puts the blame on herself. When their divorce became public—her husband leaked it to the Silicon Valley gossip pages to promote his new project—Margo expected expressions of sympathy, which are often pity in another garb. Instead, she got applause. She says that all her friends—and her entire family—celebrated the breakup. Nobody cared for her husband, and they all saw how nasty and egocentric he was. The public façade that she had struggled to keep up had never worked. The people who had no stake in this marriage saw it for what it was—a sham.

Five years after the divorce, with a new beau, a career that is back on track, and teenage children who are coming around and showing her some love and respect, Margo, who blamed herself for her miserable marriage, now blames herself for having waited so long to get out. She calls herself a fool. She is full of regret.

During the decades of her unhappy marriage, Margo underwent serious character changes. Lying to others over time makes you lie to yourself. And then you lose yourself in the web of deceit. You lose a certain closeness with your children, too, who blame you for things that aren't your fault. Because of the decision to cover up for her husband, Margo could not share with her children a fundamental truth about the emotional price she paid on their behalf. If you let your children think you're always okay, then you can't expect them to have empathy for your suffering, and you cannot expect gratitude for the sacrifice that created the life you provided them.

So by staying in the marriage for the children, Margo attenuated her relationship with them. This issue arises when unhappy parents decide not to divorce. You might sacrifice for the kids, but, in the words of a cynic, "No good deed goes unpunished."

Part II

THE BOOK OF RESOLUTIONS

5

THE LITTLE DETECTIVES

*How discovering a family secret
changes a child's character for life*

Children watch their parents with a concentration that is hard to match. They notice everything, but their interpretation of events can be mistaken. That's because they lack the information they need in order to understand what they observe. Still, children do try to fit events into patterns that make sense. Indeed, making sense of the world is a major task that begins at birth and continues throughout life. We're all still working on it.

What makes secrets so hard on children who are good observers is that when they discover the truth, they may not be able to fathom its meaning. They might have the facts, but they almost certainly lack the context. Their logic is childish, their explanations are often incorrect, and they arrive at odd conclusions. Moreover, kids have a way of putting themselves in the middle of every situation and blaming themselves for every misfortune. It's not because they have outsize consciences. It's because they begin life at the center of their universe and only gradually step aside and let the rest of the world in.

In the course of writing this book, I found a type of child I call "the little detective." When he thinks something is off-kilter, this kind of child needs to find out what's happening, and he often does find clues that lead him closer to the truth. In a family that harbors a little detective, the other children may not have much interest in searching for the facts and even less of a desire to deal with them. Where do the curiosity and the energy to follow clues to a solution of the mystery come from? That poses a chicken-and-egg problem. Which comes first, the personality that needs to know the truth, or the suspicious situation that turned a child into a detective? I'm not sure, but being a little detective can have a lifelong effect on the way these people handle difficult realities, the raw material of secrets, for the rest of their lives. That lifelong impact is on display in the stories that follow.

We begin with Brian, who spent most of his life trying to find an explanation for the clues that he picked up on the weekend before his father died. As a child, he searched for years to understand the behavior of the adults in his life, and in the process he grew from a little detective into a journalist and activist.

What Brian Knew

Brian was twelve when his father died—of pneumonia. His parents had separated several years before. His father had undergone several hospitalizations for depression over the years, and the separation came immediately after one of them. Brian spent every other weekend with his dad, whom he adored and who loved Brian and Brian's brother deeply. One Sunday, Brian was in the kitchen when the phone rang. His mother didn't use the phone much, and so the sound of the telephone came as a surprise. Brian picked up the receiver. "My aunt asked if my mother was home." Also strange. She never called to talk to his mother. So he went to fetch her. His father had been found unconscious that morning and rushed to the hospital with a terrible case of pneumonia, Brian had been told. "My mother picked up the phone and then she ushered me out of the kitchen." She closed the door. Brian put his ear to the keyhole.

"I heard 'hospital,' " he recalls. "I heard 'pills.' And I knew."

His father died on the following Wednesday.

Brian's father was moody and short-tempered with his wife. His parents' marriage was a series of long fights and brief reconciliations. There was yelling and hitting and everything a kid hates to see happening between his parents. His father had confided some of his sorrows in his son. "I knew that he took pills because he'd shown me where he kept them. And I knew that he was on an anxiety medication." This was Brian's first clue.

What Brian surmised that Sunday morning was never discussed. Brian instinctively knew not to bring it up, and he was well into his teens when he first spoke of his suspicions. At twelve, Brian had recently started at a new middle school, and he had not developed the kind of friends he could confide in. When he went back, "I didn't even tell anyone my father had died." He couldn't give the party line that his dad died of pneumonia "because I knew it was a lie." He was isolated at school as well as at home. "I kept the secret, too, because I didn't know what to say." Brian continues, "Years later, one of my friends asked me how my dad was. We hadn't talked about him in a long time." His friend had never known the truth. The loss of his father, whom he adored, would have been tough enough. But when Brian figured out the fact of his father's suicide, and had nobody to talk with, he was overwhelmed with sorrow and questions.

Then other important people in Brian's life disappeared. "It was as if a curtain came down." His dad's best friend, who had painted a portrait of his father that hung in the living room, arrived. "He came a week after my dad died—it was Christmas. He handed me a football. He took the portrait."

"Do you want to talk to my mother?" Brian asked.

"No," said the friend. And he walked out. Brian never saw him again.

Then his uncle, his father's brother, stopped coming by. "I had been very close to my uncle as a child, very close, as close as a nephew and uncle could be. And I felt such a sense of betrayal when he disappeared." Brian didn't know why. "You don't know when you're that age."

Brian became adept at keeping his questions to himself, but his feelings erupted from time to time, not always with happy results. Some years after his father's death, Brian was missing his smart, funny, handsome, loving dad. He mentioned to his mother how much he loved and missed him. His mother said, "You think he was so nice? He had an affair with so-and-so, and he did this, and he did that." So now another truth emerged. Brian's father had multiple affairs, and they were no secret to his wife.

Brian didn't know why his parents fought so much until that conversation, but the fact that they fought was undeniable. "My parents had a violent marriage, and they both had terrible tempers, and there was all kinds of physical abuse." At the point when his father was admitted to the hospital, the marriage was in deep trouble. Brian now put more pieces together.

Another element added to his misery, something Brian thought up himself. He felt responsible for his father's suicide. "Knowing that my mother was planning to change the locks on the apartment, and that she was going to ask for a divorce, I wished him dead because I couldn't imagine the explosion that was to come." Brian remembers his profound guilt. "So I thought bad things were coming, so I was just hoping for him to die." Brian blamed himself for events that were totally beyond his control. That is common when children witness discord between their parents, and in fact it is not unusual for the children to feel guilt when someone dies, whatever the circumstances. We often find ways to take some of the responsibility for a tragedy in the family. This tendency has its root in infancy.

When babies cry, they get attention, and they gradually come to think that they are the cause of everything else that happens, too. Similarly, older children blame themselves for family misfortunes like divorce or illness. This is largely due to what I call the egocentric fallacy: If I (baby) make a fuss over something I need, I'll get it, which translates into if something bad happens, it must be because of me (child). That's why it is so important for adults to help children understand, as they grow up, that they are not responsible for things over which they have no control. They also need to be reminded that thoughts don't cause events.

Gradually, over the years, Brian's father's backstory emerged. "It was kept secret that my dad was mentally ill." His father's family knew about it, and knew that other relatives suffered from depression. They hid the facts from the woman he was going to marry. Brian's mother had no idea what she was getting into. She thought she was marrying a stable, funny, handsome man. Her husband certainly was handsome, and he had a wonderful sense of fun, but Brian's mother later discovered that her husband was prone to serious depressions and had a talent for philandering.

Brian also learned over time why so many people disappeared from his life after his father's death. They blamed his mother for the suicide. She had thrown her husband out of the house because of his affairs and temper, and had asked him to leave immediately after one of his hospitalizations—when he was at his weakest. Once he'd killed himself, they blamed her for not having taken him back, believing that if she had, he would not have overdosed and died. Now Brian began to see why his mother was reticent. She didn't want to deal with her role in the events. Decades later, Brian's uncle, the one who disappeared, opened up to Brian, but only in small doses. He couldn't bear to talk about his brother's death for more than a few minutes because he became terribly upset every time he thought about it. Brian learned that this uncle had gone into a major depression when he reached the age of fifty-one, the age at which Brian's dad died. These anniversary events are not uncommon when a relative dies at a young age.

The lifetime of detective work had a powerful impact on Brian's relationships. The most important person to Brian, and the one who remained his best friend to the end of her life, was his father's mother. "We adored each other." His grandmother and Brian were always close, starting from when he was a child. He can still picture her beautiful hands and the colorful nail polish she wore. His paternal grandparents always looked out for Brian, the first grandchild in their family. When Brian was working his way through college, his grandmother saved quarters and dollars from her grocery money and gave them to him. Those saved coins mounted up and allowed him to eat decently during college.

As Brian reached his twenties, he broached the subject of his father's death at the dinner table one night. His grandmother was relieved to have that conversation. And after that, "she and I talked about my dad's suicide all the time." The two of them had been in the same spot. "She had no one to talk to. I had no one to talk to."

When Brian decided to attend graduate school in journalism his tuition was paid for by the government—he qualified for G.I. Bill of Rights benefits because of his father's service.

Then, as he began to integrate the tragedies of his life, Brian became an advocate for other people whose lives were touched by suicide. He wanted to help survivors live through the pain. Just to give you a sense of the denial in his home, when he told his mother about the book he was writing, she asked, "How come you're writing a book about suicide?"

When, years later, he found his father's letters to his brother and to his best friend, Brian learned how much his father had loved his sons, and how he had longed to be with them again. He learned of his father's anguish at the depression that overcame him. He found out that his father had hoped somehow to be reunited with his wife.

Fortunately, Brian still had his grandmother with whom to talk things over. She spoke of her guilt about her son's suicide. "We talked about it often, and went over the same things again and again. And I reassured her about what mental illness is." They became closer as he reached full adulthood and she reached old age. They spoke on the telephone for as much as forty-five minutes a day. They took vacations together and would settle themselves on the bed in her hotel room and talk over their day.

But Brian had one more shock to endure. And still he cannot deal with it. It wasn't until his grandmother was ninety-six that the whole truth emerged, by which time she was confined to her home.

"Your dad wrote a letter," she said.

"What letter?"

"Well, he wrote a letter to your mother . . ."

This happened during the separation. His father was living with his parents. He was just out of the psychiatric hospital. Grandma continued.

"He wrote a letter to your mother, and he spelled out everything he had done, with all of these women, and apologized and begged for her forgiveness." He wanted his wife to take him back.

"What did my mother say?"

"I couldn't give her that letter," his grandmother said.

"So what did you do with it?"

She had torn it up.

Brian tells me that he nearly passed out. "Because, oh my God, what if my mother had read the letter? What if my mother would have taken him back? Maybe he might not have killed himself."

Brian tried to comfort himself as we spoke. "She was ninety-six years old, and I was aware that she was unburdening herself." But he was thinking to himself, "Oh my God!" Brian learned a little bit more in that conversation. His grandmother always blamed his mother for her son's troubles. It's common to side with your own child when there is discord in a marriage.

"I couldn't let him tell your mother those things," she said, meaning his adultery.

Brian's grandmother had decided to protect her son's reputation. It may have cost her son his life. Brian respected his grandmother's age and her reluctance to tell him more, but to this day, "It takes my breath away. I didn't write about it in my suicide book, because it's unbelievable."

The shock of this revelation still gives Brian the chills, and he probably could have done without his grandmother's confession. But their relationship, which began when Brian was a child, and the intimacy of their many conversations had supported both of them over the years. Shared secrets and intimacy are twins. If you have one, you have the other. Brian's intimacy with his grandmother would not be severed by that last terrible revelation. But the confession still haunts him.

Deathbed confessions are the worst kind of bombshell. Any benefits, it is worth noting, are more for the dying than for the living. These late truths can burden the stunned survivors for the rest of their lives.

In Sara's story, as in Brian's, we see how strong and supple the bond of intimacy can be when it grows out of candor. Sara, too, was a little detective, and her relationship of honesty with her mother served as a shield when she discovered some difficult truths.

Sara Asks Twenty Questions

Whenever Sara asked her mother a direct question, she got a truthful reply. This tradition began when Sara was a little girl. She noticed that the tooth fairy's handwriting was very much like her mom's. So she asked, "Is the tooth fairy real?"

Her mother shook her head. "No."

"Santa Claus?"

Headshake.

"Easter Bunny?"

Same thing.

Sara was clued in and glued to her mom forever because she knew she could trust her to answer any question she asked. Perhaps because her mother grew up in a family where everybody kept secrets from everybody else, she adopted this strategy with her first child, a daughter with whom she has remained close. Sara believes that her relationship with her mom helped her to grow up with a greater understanding of other people.

Sara, today in her early twenties, recalls a moment when her mom seemed very sad. "I was about thirteen years old, so I was just at the age when I could suspect that things were going on, and I was also of the age when, if it was to be explained to me, I would understand it in a more mature way than I might if I were a child." Her mom cried a lot, and Sara noticed a certain distance between her parents. "I was very, very nosy." She would ask her mom, "What's going on? Tell me what's going on." She picked up on little cues. She remembers her parents sitting out on a hammock having what looked like a really disappointing conversation. The situation between them began to deteriorate. "It was during that time that my mom began to take refuge with me, and she would sleep in my bed sometimes, and she would cry in my bed."

Sara remembers the night her world fell apart. Her mom was in her bed, and she said, "We're going to get a divorce. I'm asking Dad to leave the house tomorrow, so he's going to move out into an apartment."

Sara and her mom fell back on their tradition of twenty questions.

"Is it about Dad?"

"Yes."

"Did he do something?"

"Yes."

"Did he cheat on you?"

"Well, yes, in a way."

"Who did he cheat on you with?"

"You don't know her."

At this point, our little detective stopped the game, which had turned sad and frightening. "I was angry. I was very, very sad. I was very disappointed. All of a sudden I felt like my father was not who I thought he was." Sara was a wise child, so she didn't immediately think, "I hate you, Dad! I hate you!" or "I want you out of my life! You hurt my mom!" Sara didn't take that position because it just didn't feel right. Sara, like so many kids in her situation, continued to love her father, even though he had betrayed her mother. "My dad had never done anything to me."

Little detectives keep their eyes and ears open, whether or not the secret keepers think they are being watched. Soon after the separation, Sara saw for herself what her father was doing. He took Sara and her sister on a ski trip and one night he left the cabin to put out the trash. He took a very long time to come back. "I remember looking out the window and seeing him on his cell phone, and I was just like, he's talking to a woman. I knew it, I knew it then, and I remember that night after he came back in—he thought we were all asleep—he was on the phone in the condo, and I had my ear to the door." Sara heard something like, "I think I'm falling for you."

She had a double reaction, one that is common among children who have been deceived. Now that her parents were separated, Sara felt loyalty to her mother, thinking, "How could you do that to Mom?"

Then, seeing that he couldn't stop being with the new woman even while he was supposed to be focusing on his daughters, Sara was hurt and thought, "How could you do that to me?"

Why couldn't her father check his romantic impulses for one measly weekend with his kids? This pattern of deceit and discovery continued. Sara's father moved to his own apartment, swearing up and down that he didn't have a girlfriend. One day when Sara and her little sister were there alone, they found a box of tampons in the bathroom. It didn't belong to Sara. That was a good clue. Then, when they spied a lacy nightie lodged in the corner of the foldout bed, they knew there must be a lady in his life. It was not a big surprise when he married this woman, whom they despised. They couldn't imagine how he could prefer her to their mom. Over the next months, they found out the answer to that question. By this time Sara's little sister had become her detective sidekick.

"Sara, I know where Dad keeps the key to his marijuana," she said. Sara was fourteen, just experiencing marijuana for the first time. Her initial thought was about how valuable his stash was.

"Where is it?" Sara whispered.

"It's in her jewelry box."

"How do you know?"

Her little sister had been spying. She peeked into the study and saw her dad's wife put a key into a drawer. Sara was proud of her. "She was my sidekick. She was my Dr. Watson!" So Sara opened the drawer and found the pot. But she got more than she bargained for. "I also found these crazy sex toys and porn. I remember picking up this long thing, and I was like, 'What is this?'" It was a dildo.

Once again, Sara'd had enough. So she stole some of his pot and began a period when she completely disrespected her father's privacy. She enjoyed the pot, but she wasn't happy with herself or with her father's secrets.

By the time Sara was sixteen, one final bit of information about her father emerged. As she rooted around in the secret drawer, Sara found a website address. "Hmm, why would he hide this?" So she went online and typed in the address. "It comes up on this swinger website." Revolted, Sara at last understood what her father saw in his new wife. She was interested in sexual activities that Sara's mother was not. The big question was answered, but Sara's feelings about her father were still unresolved.

Eventually, like many people who are shocked and miserable about revelations that shake their world, Sara came to terms with her dad. "From a very early time I had to separate the way I feel about him as a father and all of these things that I know about him as a man. I just really love him a lot, unconditionally, because he raised me, and he cared for me, and he loves me. I know he has a lot of problems, and as someone who is a healthier person than he is, I can see and understand a lot of his problems, and I can see him in denial. I can see all these things, but that does not take away the fact that I love him."

Sara's mother deserves credit for helping her daughter keep a positive view of her father. "She was always truthful to me while still trying to protect my own image of my father as having always been a good father to me," Sara says. "When I think of my dad in my childhood, I think of him reading to me every single night before going to bed and playing with me and being goofy and silly."

Sara had some difficult years between the revelations and coming to terms with them. She got into serious drugs and dropped out of college. Her mother couldn't deal with her, despite their closeness (or perhaps because of it), and Sara was shipped off to her father. She lived with him and the hated wife for a while, and then went into rehab. This was not a good time for anybody, but eventually Sara came through it. She went back to college and now loves school. She is articulate, funny, and clear about how she feels. Her relationship with her mother continues to be close and loving. They have great admiration for each other. And she has found a way to stay close to her dad, too. They keep to subjects that don't raise red flags. "We don't talk about matters that are close to the heart or to the genitals."

For both Brian and Sara, learning that their instincts were good and that their suspicions were accurate gave them confidence in their own judgment. That confidence is often helpful when you have to face painful facts, realities you would just as soon not have to deal with.

Parents keep secrets to protect themselves and their children. When the truth comes out, both parent and child have an opportunity to work through tough realities. Sometimes we grow when we face facts together, and sometimes we have to survive hard times in order to gain perspective on one another and our pasts.

There is a particular advantage for parents who decide to be honest with their children. Since we all fill in the blanks according to what we already believe about the world, and since teenagers still have an incomplete understanding of adult behavior and the ins and outs of families, truthful conversations give parents the opportunity to offer their points of view where a destructive one might otherwise take root.

Brian's penchant for the truth turned him into a journalist. Learning secrets had shaped his character profoundly. Sara's closeness with her mother was the foundation of her capacity to see and to understand. She could trust her mother to tell her the truth, and that made truth her friend, not a stranger. This offered Sara the ability to find out the facts and deal with them, and it has helped her understand and stay close to her father.

Amanda, too, was an observant child and is now an adult who respects the power of truth, no matter how difficult it may be. Her path has not been easy, but she moves along it with strength and love.

What Amanda Knew

Amanda's parents fought the old-fashioned way, yelling and screaming and slamming doors. She and her sisters headed to the closet in a distant part of the house and cowered as they closed the door to block out the words. But on this evening the raging battle was too loud. They heard their father accuse their mother of having an affair with his law partner and close friend. Someone had spotted them having an intimate dinner in a fancy restaurant.

"You're sleeping with him," Amanda's father said. "I know it."

Then Amanda and her sister heard their mother's reply.

"That's PRE-posterous."

Amanda's response was sophisticated for an eight-year-old child. "My mother used the word 'preposterous.'" That was the tip-off. "She's lying." Amanda knew it. If her mother were telling the truth she would have denied the affair, not the accusation.

Amanda was not surprised. She had been onto her mother's secret life for some time. "We were out at the lake, she would go on a drive for an hour, and I was just a very savvy kid, and I thought she's not driving to watch the dogwood, which was where she said she was going. I actually thought that she was meeting somebody." The affair, which ended soon after the argument, did not break up Amanda's parents' marriage. They gradually started to get closer and there was never a whiff of adultery from then on.

Amanda is the youngest of three daughters. The eldest was

her father's favorite, the middle sister was her mother's favorite, and Amanda was pretty much left to fend for herself. There are two sides to being the child who gets the least attention. On the one hand it can be lonely, and such children often wish they were at the center of the family. On the other hand that sense of being on your own can foster a degree of independence and self-reliance. Some kids learn to trust their own judgment in the absence of parental focus and grow up to rely on themselves. That's Amanda, a sculptor whose work graces public spaces in cities around the world. She credits her position in the family for her independence of mind and her determination.

Amanda's childhood was peppered with illness, and it was when she got sick that her mother paid her the attention she craved. Amanda's mom was an elegant and energetic woman, beautiful, sexy, smart, an effective hostess, and a flirt. A magazine editor and writer who specialized in beautiful homes, she had impeccable taste. Amanda never seems to have become ill at a convenient time for her mother. Her appendix burst the day her mother was launching a new magazine, and her mom spent the next few weeks at Amanda's bedside as she fought peritonitis. Amanda always wondered if she got sick to get her mother's attention. When I commented that I had never heard of a psychosomatic burst appendix, she laughed.

Amanda's gratitude to her mother makes her eyes fill with tears as she tells me how her mother came to her aid when Amanda was in graduate school, how she moved into her university apartment and helped her sick daughter through the oral exams and through the vetting of her dissertation. Amanda connected her physical problems with her mom's help, and so when she was having trouble conceiving and her first attempt at in vitro fertilization failed, she once again longed for that intimacy.

By this time Amanda was married and it was not appropriate to ask her mother to move in. But she wanted to clear up the childhood mystery, perhaps in order to reconnect with her mother as she had years before, when she was sick. She made a phone call.

"I'm really, really terribly depressed after losing this baby," she said. "I don't know why this is on my mind, but I just have to ask you: Did you have an affair with X?"

There was a silence. And her mother said, "Yes. I did."

It was a huge relief. Amanda's suspicion all those years ago was right. Then she learned more about her parents' long-ago marriage. It was rocky for many reasons, including alcohol and her father's dark moods. Amanda's mother had been suffering, and she had warned her husband: "If you don't get some counseling, with or without me, or if we don't do something, I'm afraid I'm going to have an affair."

This revelation led to a longer conversation, which offered Amanda a way to understand her mother's behavior. The connection between Amanda and her mother began to change, and gradually they became closer and more relaxed together.

Secrets kept over years have a tendency to separate people. When the truth is shared, even tacitly, tensions may fade. That's what Amanda experienced with her mom. She kept these insights with her as she faced the next set of decisions about truth versus lies, under much more trying circumstances. This is the second chapter of Amanda's encounter with secrecy. Her response, which took courage, was formed by her childhood as a little detective.

The Secrets Amanda Tells

Amanda's efforts to get pregnant eventually failed, and so she and her husband adopted a baby girl from a couple who were together, but not married, and in financial trouble. When the same couple had another child, the birth mother offered the next baby to Amanda and her husband for adoption, which is how they got their son. Now they had a complete family. For someone who'd spent decades suspecting the truth without knowing for sure, Amanda has a clear preference for transparency. She dealt with the children as honestly and simply as she could, in an age-appropriate way, telling them that they were adopted and that they had the same mother and father.

Amanda maintained a relationship of sorts with the biological mother—they exchanged holiday cards, and Amanda sent her annual photos of the kids. This level of contact came easily to her, as it often does to adoptive parents who know the birth parents and want to keep things on an even keel. Amanda also knew that the couple had kept their first child, a son, but she did not tell her children about their older brother. She felt confident in the decision, thinking it would be hard for such young children to understand why their mother had kept her first child and given them away. Adopted kids often suffer abandonment issues, and Amanda thought that the pain would be magnified if they knew about their older brother. Her confidence did not last for long.

When the birth mother announced to Amanda that she was pregnant again, by the same man, but planned to keep this baby, Amanda felt horrible. "When am I going to tell them?" How could she explain this to her kids? Here was a puzzle that Amanda, for all her brilliance and insight, couldn't solve. She talked with her husband, her therapist, and her friends. But nobody could help her find a way to explain to her kids that their birth mother kept her first and last children, and had given them—the two middle children—away. It's one thing to offer children a context in which to understand a complex situation, but it's quite another to come up with an explanation for behavior she knew would hurt her kids. Amanda was stumped.

Even though truth and transparency are a huge point of principle for Amanda, she kept the new baby a secret for almost eighteen months, feeling torn all the time. She was violating her principle of openness and yet she couldn't see how to explain to her children their birth mother's decisions in a way that did not exacerbate their sense of abandonment. She wanted to come clean, but like so many secret keepers, she would look for the right moment and then put it off. Then social media did what Amanda could not bear to do.

Here's where Amanda's story becomes complicated and sad. And here is where Amanda's instinct for transparency may have made things harder for her and the children. The birth mother "friended" Amanda on Facebook. She felt obliged to accept.

Then about a year later, when her daughter was ten, Amanda had her Facebook page up. While her attention was elsewhere, Amanda's daughter, a second-generation little detective, recognized her birth mother's name among the list of friends.

"That's my birth mother," she said.

"Yes, it is."

"Can I go on her page?"

Amanda felt she had no alternative. "Yes. You can."

And so Amanda and her daughter saw the older brother, the one the birth mother had kept. "He looked exactly like my son." And then they saw a picture of a little baby.

"Who's this baby?"

Amanda told her. Then her daughter started to ask questions that Amanda couldn't answer, questions that amounted to *why?*

"I'll e-mail her to find out," she said.

So Amanda sent a message to the birth mother.

"The children found out, I just have a couple of questions." She didn't get much of an answer. They kept this baby because they could. Amanda was miserable. "My daughter adores children, and adores little girls." She would constantly ask Amanda, "Are you going to adopt another baby? Let's have another baby."

The revelation via social media brought up the same questions and regrets her children felt when they found out they had been adopted. Seeing the pictures of the children their birth parents kept was painful. It brought home the reality of their adoption—and abandonment—in a new way.

"Why did she give us away and keep the other children?"

"This happens," Amanda said. "Sometimes people actually don't have the resources, and feel that it would be better if somebody else can provide more."

Amanda watched as they took it in, both of them, gradually, painfully, and sadly.

"We're all in it together," Amanda said, as she hugged them.

When she accepted the birth mother's request to be a Facebook friend, Amanda could not have anticipated the outcome. So she lost the opportunity to delay this truth from her kids until they were older. The Facebook moment may have been a blunder, but the consequences are more consonant with Amanda's beliefs. Now they all struggle together. There's anger, and sorrow, and acting out, and school problems. But throughout her lifetime with secrets, suspected and revealed, Amanda has developed a philosophy.

"I was driving my kids to a picnic the other day, and we were trying to find a street sign, and the street sign had grown into the tree, and the tree had grown around it. And we could only see the E-R-E of Revere Road. But we knew it was Revere Road because of the end. So I feel like their consciousness just grows around it. In ways that it just reconfigures."

I asked Amanda if the kids are still curious about their siblings. "Yes. And they look at pictures on Facebook all the time. I let them. I feel like there's this thing about transparency, you can kind of go overboard with it, and I feel like there are things you can't expose your kids to, but when you get to the realm that can be transparent, it's such a relief to not have to shield this and shield that." Amanda's faith, born of struggle, gives her hope. "They'll be okay, so long as they know that I'm there, and I'm not going anywhere."

Maybe that is wishful thinking on Amanda's part, but we all live in the twenty-first century, when privacy seems to be going the way of white gloves and shoes that match the handbag. Eventually Amanda's daughter and son would have found out the truth of their birth mother's other children. Would life have been easier without Facebook? Certainly. Would her kids have been better off if their birth mother hadn't "friended" Amanda or had not posted cute pictures of the children she kept? Sure. Sadly, we can't change facts to suit our desires, and Amanda has done her best to walk the line between honesty and too much information. She believes that her children have the capacity to grow around their difficult truths, so long as they can rely on her embrace.

For Amanda, the burden of truth is lighter than the weight of secrets.

6

IF YOU SEE SOMETHING, SAY SOMETHING

*The pernicious effect of
enforced silence*

"If you see something, say something." It's a post-9/11 cliché, a simple and memorable way of reminding us that unattended packages pose a threat because we don't know what is inside. There could be a bomb. Most of these abandoned parcels contain clothing, papers, books, and other stuff of everyday life. But we dare not ignore the abandoned package. Anything mysterious and hidden is frightening. Its secret contents could destroy us. Our minds rush to the worst case. The bomb squad may disarm the package, or they may find that it is harmless. The danger fades. Once we know, the energy that attends the unknown dissipates.

You can observe a similar dynamic in some families. If an event or a fact is declared a secret—even though everybody knows it—the content turns dangerous. In these situations, the secret is hiding in plain sight. Some people call it the elephant in the room. Whatever you call it, something has happened that everybody knows about and nobody in the family is allowed to mention. The reasons for declaring a family silence over such unmentionables—death, alcohol, and illness—are understandable, but the impact is hard to bear. It isn't easy to talk about the death of a child or a crazy mom or a disability that shames the family. It hurts. Silence appears to be a good solution. But an attempt to control the anxiety, worry, or fear by declaring the subject unmentionable buries the feelings. The emotions have no place to go. They fester inside us.

I learned about this in a small way when my second husband died in 2010. Two of our grandchildren used to spend time with us every week, and they adored their Pop Pop. Benji was six and Ruby was two. Benji had questions about everything: how his grandfather looked when he died, what it felt like to hold his hand, when his breathing stopped, how they took his body away. I didn't much enjoy the conversation, but I felt an obligation to honor both the little boy's curiosity and the memory of my husband. So I told him everything. It didn't seem ghoulish to either of us. He was relieved to know the facts, and I felt better in the telling.

Years later these kids still remember their grandfather and sometimes want to talk about him. It was their first experience with death. I used to get weepy, and when Benji saw me tear up he would say, "Grandma, let's change the subject," and we did. He didn't want me to be sad, and it wasn't easy to revisit my grief. We were both relieved when we moved to other topics.

But his little sister, who was too young at the time to take this all in, sometimes still wants to talk about it because she has a lot of feeling but not much understanding.

"Pop Pop's never going to get better, is he?" she says.

"No."

"Where is he?" she asks.

"In our hearts."

"No, really?" she persists.

"In the air and the sky."

She looks up.

Then I long to change the subject, but Ruby is intent on finding out the answers to her questions and doesn't yet know that some of them are unanswerable. I respect her need to air her sad feelings and satisfy her curiosity. These talks are precious to me. I believe that they will in some way help to preserve Benji and Ruby's love for their grandfather, even though they probably will forget the details because they were so young when he died. We keep on talking. Sometimes I still cry.

These conversations have given me some understanding of why people ban sad subjects, especially with children who haven't learned what is taboo. Their questions can be hard to hear and impossible to answer. But here's the rub: You can change the subject, but you can't stop people from wondering and worrying about it.

Mountains of psychological research support this. Tell a person not to think about elephants, and those large animals will lurk at the edges of consciousness, distracting the person from concentrating on the task at hand. Daniel Kahneman, in his book *Thinking, Fast and Slow*, describes fascinating experiments showing how hard we have to work to suppress thoughts that run through our minds. What is true of universities and laboratories is true of the living room and the kitchen—we don't find it any easier there to repress or deny our feelings.

Tragedies happen. Marriages break up, relationships collapse, and people carry these burdens for life. So why bother to talk about it? Why not say, as many people do, "The subject is too painful. We will never discuss this again," and get on with life? That would make sense, except that it ignores the persistence of powerful feelings. The guilt, the pain, the anger, and the sorrow from the tragedy don't dry up and blow away. What takes the place of conversation is the creation of myths, of spurious reasons why the event happened. When the conversation does not happen, when competing versions of the event are not discussed and compared, then we are deprived of a shared reality. So the myths, which are often worse than the facts, take on the illusion of truth. We are a storytelling species, and we communicate to survive. When we can't speak together we are alone in our pain. Silence keeps us from finding comfort in each other.

There is another unintended consequence of silence. When you put bad things aside, and do your best to ignore them, you don't make it easy to feel much at all, and you lose access to your authentic self.

Henry's Menagerie

Henry still can't figure out what on earth he was thinking when he got himself into such trouble.

Henry and his wife of many years had a business together, and they were very successful. This smart and energetic couple could do no wrong in their work. They made lots of money, but they were not show-offs about it; they lived modestly. They began to grow apart a bit as their girls grew up, but they were still friends who always had interesting things to talk about and enjoyed each other's company. Henry thought everything was fine, although he knew that his wife didn't like the fact that he would walk away from conflict, preferring distance to confrontation. Perhaps he could have been more conscious of his wife's unhappiness, but he had plenty of help staying oblivious. He had started drinking, which increased their distance. Alcohol is a good tool of self-deception.

One night, his wife had gone out to pick up some dessert and was hours late coming back. Henry was ready to start calling the hospitals when she arrived home in tears.

"He's not going to leave his wife," she said.

Henry didn't know what she was talking about. Then she broke down and confessed. The man she had fallen in love with had just broken his promise to marry her. They had met on the Internet. It began innocently, but over time it became serious. They started an affair, fell in love, and planned to divorce their spouses in order to be together. That night, Henry's wife wasn't out picking up dessert; she was out getting jilted.

"She treated me as a girlfriend," Henry said with wonder. He was clear about one thing that night. "I'm not your girlfriend, I'm your husband."

It was a shock to Henry, who had been successful in keeping troubled feelings below the surface. "I had worked with great energy to keep the whipped cream whipped."

Partners in the company, they knew each other's passwords. Henry had never thought to pry. They had been a team until that night. The next day he searched her e-mails from start to finish. Then the whole story emerged. It did begin innocently, but it escalated. Devastated and furious beyond words, Henry moved out. They chose not to go into marriage counseling— she was willing, but he wasn't. And he admits that he really wasn't eager to face the secrets he had lived with all his life. As a result of the divorce, they sold the business.

And here's where Henry got into trouble. He survived the end of his marriage, but he was in a hurry to unload the company, and so he made a good deal financially but a poor one in every other way. The buyer insisted that Henry not tell anybody about the sale or that he was no longer in charge. It made sense to the buyer because everybody loved Henry and trusted him completely. Henry agreed to carry on a charade of leadership in order to conclude the negotiations and sell the company. His secrecy about the transfer of ownership was part of the contract. Then the business began to go downhill. Henry by now had left town and kept up appearances long distance. He lied to his customers about where the products they had ordered were and lied to his suppliers about why their bills were not paid. He was miserable but saw no way out. "I thought I was relieving myself of something, when in fact I was buying horrible trouble" by agreeing to keep a bunch of secrets. Henry suffered. "And there was no, no fun in that, and no gratification. It got to be a total spiderweb, in which I was caught, not catching dinner."

His lies and fabrications continued for a couple of years, and eventually he could no longer keep up the charade. When he confessed to lifelong business associates, who had become dear friends, they were hurt and angry, and dropped him from their lives. By the time Henry came clean, he had lost everything: his business, his income, and the trust of his customers and friends. Today he is trying hard to rebuild, and it isn't easy. He has faced his drinking problem and is going to Alcoholics Anonymous meetings. He founded an interesting start-up, and he discovered a love of painting, which absorbs much of his free time. Henry may well get his life back together. But it takes discipline to reform a lifelong habit of nonconfrontation. In his efforts to change, Henry has learned something. "Retreating is another form of dishonesty and an act of hiding." A longtime good friend tried to get close to him and asked, "Are you hiding out?"

"Yeah," Henry said. "I'm working toward something, but I am also hiding."

Henry is angrier with himself than he is at his former wife or the person who bought the business under such damaging conditions. He knows he made people suffer, and he knows how he suffered every day during the years he was forced to keep the secret. He is fully aware of the straits he is in. "It's very hard and very lonely. You wake up in the house alone, and I think to myself, is that noise the kids? And of course it's the wind."

Henry's candor in telling his story and his refusal to make excuses for himself made it hard for me to understand how he could have gotten himself into this spot. The deceptions and lies didn't fit with the man I was getting to know. So as the tale of deception and sorrow wound down, I asked him to tell me something about his childhood. What I heard helped me to make sense of Henry's unwise decisions.

Henry was the third child in his family. A brother and a sister came first. When he was a baby, the sister, who was ten at the time, died in one of the late polio epidemics. His mother struggled to get through each day while caring for the two surviving children—six-month-old Henry and his six-year-old brother. She was desolate. Henry tells me that his brother had an especially hard time. For him, the unspoken message was, "Why did she have to die, instead of you?" He was burdened with survivor guilt.

What made the situation more complicated was that after the death of his sister, his parents laid down an edict of silence. Her name could never be mentioned in the house. The children (they had another daughter when Henry was three) were not allowed to ask questions about their dead sister or talk about her at all. That was hard. But in addition, Henry's parents packed all of her things in a big cabinet that sat, locked, in the living room. Imagine seeing it every day, wondering what it contained, and never being allowed to open it or talk about it. Does that remind you of an abandoned backpack on the subway?

Henry was a baby when all this happened, but he does recall a scene that he either witnessed or heard about. One night at dinner, the phone rang. Somebody who didn't know what had happened asked to speak to his sister. His mother screamed, slammed down the phone, and retreated to the bathroom for the rest of the evening.

His parents could not find a way to relieve their pain. Religion wasn't a comfort, and grief therapy was not yet common. So a kindly but stupid doctor, seeing the trouble they were in, suggested that a nice cocktail before dinner might blunt the misery. It certainly did something, because Henry's parents, who had not been drinkers, gradually became alcoholics. They drank and fought and screamed and yelled at each other every night.

They created such a ruckus that neighbor children would ask Henry what had happened at his home the night before. He lied to keep the family secret. Even though gossip migrated through his school, Henry was able to keep up appearances. He describes himself as tap-dancing through his adolescence.

Many people call alcoholic parents the elephant in the room. You can't discuss it, you have to tiptoe around it, and you can never predict when things are going to get out of hand. It is scary, and it eats into your ability to relax. But the silence in the face of his sister's death did special damage. It left the surviving children with a residue of sadness and guilt, which was never expunged.

Henry's early training prepared him to make the agreements and keep the secrets that got him into trouble later in life. He had become a superb fabricator. His charm and eloquence could help him cover up whatever he didn't want people to know. He also became a master at ignoring what he felt. He began to live on the surface because as a boy he had been trained to ignore the option of going deeper. Only now, after losing almost everything, has Henry started to face his dark feelings, his bad acts. He is at the start of a process that may help him become authentic, which is the basis of a decent life. It may be that through the next few years Henry will not only accept his sadness and his guilt but also reacquaint himself with his charm and intelligence, and his love of life, and his creativity. He may begin to discover his true self. That is the hope.

For Henry, even though he saw something, he absolutely could not say something. Under this edict of silence, there was no way to temper the family's pain, to explain the pervasive sorrow. There was no way to bond with his siblings or connect with his parents. And the imposed silence he experienced as a child set the stage for a life that stayed on the surface. Only now, after the devastation of his divorce and the loss of his reputation, is Henry beginning to face himself and starting to rebuild.

Anne also grew up in a house where the most obvious fact was denied and ignored. Her mother, a polio victim, had been paralyzed since she was a child. She was confined to a wheelchair long before Anne was born. Anne's parents and grandparents had long ago made a pact of denial. Her mother had no disability. She was just like everybody else and her life was fine. She grew up to be a gracious hostess, a fine musician, happily married with two lovely children. Everything was just fine. Except it wasn't. The vow of silence begun by Anne's grandparents sealed the family into a degree of falseness and pain that migrated across the generations.

The Wheelchair in the Room
This book is my attempt to make sense of the
legacy of my mother's illness and the price all of
us paid for not speaking the truth.
—Anne, *The Polio Journals*

Anne grew up in a beautiful, light-filled home in Los Angeles. Hers was a privileged life. Her father was an accountant, her mother a musician. They had maids and big parties, and she and her older brother went horseback riding every weekend with their father.

Her mother was a bit of a celebrity in their social circle. This brilliant and accomplished harpsichordist and concert artist was a paragon of elegance and charm. There was one small problem: She was paralyzed from the waist down. She had contracted polio when she was a child, and by the time Anne was born, her mother was confined to a wheelchair. Her mother's positive attitude and energy formed the basis of her persona. But even though the fact of her disability was obvious to everybody, it could never be discussed. Never. If the word "polio" were mentioned, "my mother would look the other way, an angry expression on her face." Anne soon learned the unspoken rule of silence at home. "We were never to think of our family, or our mother, as being limited in ways that others weren't."

Anne grew up in an elegant version of the fun house. Everything was distorted. It was a modern home, designed without staircases so Anne's mother could easily navigate. But small things made it hard for her mother. The kitchen had not been designed with a wheelchair-bound woman in mind, so she could not reach the cabinets or use the counter. Sometimes she would scream in frustration.

Her mother was noble and heroic in many ways. But "the constant accolades from those around me about how wonderful and courageous my mother was conflicted with my own feelings of shame surrounding her and me." When parents decide to ignore the most important fact in the family and impose an edict of silence, everybody suffers. Kids make up all kinds of explanations for the disparity between what they see and what they are told to believe. Talking about what is going on in your life is vital to all people. It's the way we get the reassurance and nurturing we need. Kids in Anne's situation need more, not less, conversation and reassurance. The silence was meant to give Anne and her brother a sense of normalcy. But for Anne it had the opposite effect. Her family wanted to believe that her mother's polio was inconsequential. Instead of ignoring her mother's paralysis, she did the opposite. Anne "inadvertently came to believe that the only way to feel loved by my mother was to focus on her paralysis." Not only did Anne feel pity for her, knowing that her disability was a sad and regrettable occurrence, but she felt guilt as well. She was "experiencing [my mother's] painful feelings as if they were my own, as well as guilt that I could do things she could not."

Imagine being able to skip around the room, to jump and dance. Imagine the joy that such freedom offers. Now imagine wanting to skip and dance and jump for your mother, watching for her delight. Now imagine wanting to skip and dance in front of a mother in a wheelchair. Would the guilt over your ability and her disability short-circuit your joy? Anne developed a strategy for dealing with this: She unconsciously adopted "magical thinking" and came to believe that if she took up "the burdens of shouldering my mother's unspoken feelings about her paralysis, I could lighten the intensity of her sadness."

Guilt over the sorrows of people you love comes naturally to many of us, and one way to deal with that would have been to talk—with somebody in the family. Anne never had such conversations. "Without any information from her regarding her paralysis, I had no sense of when to worry about her and when not to, so I became consumed with her well-being."

So instead of freeing her daughter, Anne's mother bound her daughter even more tightly to her pain. If Anne went out, her mother would turn her face away from the goodbye kiss. She hated to be alone. If Anne had friends over, she was on tenterhooks, praying that her mother's disability would not spoil their fun. She had witnessed the way people in wheelchairs, including her mother, were mistreated in stores and restaurants and other public places. It was difficult for Anne to square her experience with the script at home: "We are a normal family and we will brook no contradictions about it."

Anne was aware of the tensions between her mother and father, even though they projected love and warmth to the world. After the elegant parties, her parents would enjoy one last cocktail and recap the evening. Sometimes they would joke about the guests, and other times they would luxuriate in the fun of the party. This balance of intimacy and aggression was part of her parents' relationship. Her father was patient and kind to his wife, and Anne cannot remember a request he didn't respond to with anything less than genuine caring. But her mother's ease in the world would disappear when her father went out. She was frightened to be alone. She could deal with it when he took the kids horseback riding on weekends, but they fought when he went out to play tennis or to meet his friends. Things got tense when he left town for board meetings of the charity he was devoted to. Once Anne heard her mother threaten to kill herself if he left her for the weekend. His response was characteristic. He shrugged and packed his bag, and he arranged for a friend to stay with her. Silence is a powerful tool. It keeps people from resolving their differences with amity. It adds tension to even simple events.

Anne's story of growing up in such an odd situation is exceptionally painful. But there was another chapter to this tale. After her mother's death, Anne's father presented her with the journals her mother had kept for most of her life. Her mother had kept the journals a secret, but she willed them to her daughter. There Anne found the real woman in the wheelchair. All her mother's pain, passion, and misery lay in those pages. Once she read the journals, Anne wanted to talk with the whole family about their shared but unspoken experience. And she decided to write a book in which she would interweave her experiences with her mother's writings. The book, *The Polio Journals*, is illuminating and heartbreaking, and it is about the power that secrets have to mutilate a family.

Anne writes, "I now know that my willingness to believe that my mother's paralysis was insignificant was a means of protecting myself from my own childhood scars, brought on by growing up in a family bound by secrets, forbidden to express pain."

Anne decided to interview all her relatives in preparation for the book. One of her close relatives, who was in and out of Anne's house all the time, asked, "What is polio anyway?"

Anne was surprised. "You don't know what polio is?"

"Is that a virus?"

Anne's uncle, her mother's brother, was especially warm and helpful. He told her family stories and provided whatever backup he had. His wife didn't approve. She would walk by the room where they sat, stick her head into the doorway, and glare.

"Anne," she said, "why do you have to do this? Why can't you just let it go?"

"I want to honor a part of my mother that has never been honored."

And then her aunt gave her what they used to call the Cut Direct: "You know if I saw that on a book jacket in a bookstore, I would never buy it."

The reactions of this couple mirrored Anne's own experience: When there is openness, there can be warmth. Silence, when threatened by questions, evokes levels of sorrow and anger. When she left their apartment, Anne thought, "Boy, this is what my mother was under all the time." She gradually gained insight into her mother's true circumstances. Her mother didn't dare talk with her family. She could just as easily evoke rage as compassion. Anne was reminded of a long-ago conversation with her grandfather. He told her how, despite all the ways in which he had tried to help his daughter, their relationship had remained strained for decades. "His shoulders drooped and his head lowered as tears streamed down his face. I was at a loss as to how I might comfort him, but I know exactly what he meant."

The book she researched and wrote was Anne's portal into her mother's experience. And here's what she found.

The Little Poster Girl

Take a moment and pull up March of Dimes posters on the Internet. You will see pictures of beautiful little girls in braces, on crutches, and in wheelchairs. On one poster a little girl on crutches with leg braces is smiling up at Elvis Presley. She looks ecstatic. All the children on all these posters are beaming. That's the way a child with infantile paralysis was expected to look and behave: Smile and be grateful for what you have. These posters will break your heart. Anne's mother, Carol, knew the script and played her part all her life.

Stricken with a frightening and mysterious disease when she was two and a half, Carol, a pretty and smart little girl, lost the use of her legs. People at that time did not know whether such paralysis was permanent, and so for many years, she labored to be able to walk again. She disappointed herself and others because her efforts were futile. But she suffered more than just disappointment. The early treatments included sessions in which she experienced exceptionally painful stretching and pulling. She trained herself not to cry. She underwent multiple surgeries. She trained herself not to complain. She spent months in body casts, itching and miserable. She showed only gratitude for the attention of others.

Her mother, horrified by her daughter's plight and suffering the shame that came with disability, could barely look at her. She took Carol to the hospital for her surgery and waited until it was over. But then her mother went home and didn't visit Carol during the months she spent in the hospital. Her mother's absence stayed with Carol for the rest of her life. She wrote that when she was home, she would wait all alone in her bedroom until she heard her father's key in the front door. Then she knew she would get some love. Her father would read to his little girl until she fell asleep. If he didn't appear, her night was restless and sad.

Her parents were fierce in their efforts to help Carol. In the early 1930s they shipped her, now just about three years old, to a place called Warm Springs, Georgia, which specialized in treating patients with infantile paralysis. Her mother couldn't bear to come, so Carol's aunt accompanied her for the months-long stay. Carol missed her mother, but it was a good place for her. Surrounded by children and adults who were also paralyzed, Carol could relax and have the fun that all children deserve. Swimming in warm water was part of the therapy, but it was also a wonderful release—she could glide through the water with ease, freed for a brief time from the heavy braces and the burden of limbs that didn't work.

During that first stay, she made friends with a charismatic young politician who was also taking the cure. He took a special shine to Carol. They had neighboring cabins, and after dinner, he would invite Carol and her aunt to his cottage. The adults played bridge, and Carol fell asleep on her aunt's lap. The politician was Franklin Delano Roosevelt, and his companion was Missy LeHand. When he was elected president, he made sure that Carol and her family were invited to the 1933 inauguration. The affection and encouragement Roosevelt offered Carol, and the sense of being accepted, warmed her for the rest of her life. Reading this passage, Anne understood the significance of the autographed picture of FDR in Carol's study. Her mother had never uttered a word about it. She never mentioned anything that had to do with her polio. Only in her journal did Carol confide the truth about her life.

Here's an example of good intentions and poor execution. When her parents built a swimming pool for Carol at their country house, they neglected to think of how hard it is for a child in braces to get up and down the stairs. So in order to swim, which she loved, she had to negotiate steep stairs. No complaints from Carol. They chose an outstanding college with a hilly and bucolic campus. Carol navigated a country setting and remarked how grateful she was when a class met on the ground floor of a building.

She maintained her stoicism in front of everybody, even her most intimate friends and relatives. Only in her journal could she rage over the cruelties she experienced. She fought with herself over the falseness of her façade. Friends in California, where she and her family lived this "perfect" life, never had any idea of what the witty and warm Carol was thinking about them. This is what she confided in her journal:

> I am ruthless, judgmental, furious with people who pretend. I want to rub people's noses in their truths, in their painful truths. Only if they acknowledge their truths can I, do I, have compassion. I don't like this in me; I think it's ugly. It's almost malevolent.

Carol was able to manage much of the physical pain—at least until the time when it returned savagely toward the end of her life—but the emotional pain roiled and bubbled on. She felt dependent on her husband and not fully loved. She suspected that he had married her for her parents' money. And she knew that she had to be gracious and grateful for the sacrifices he made to marry her. She had no way to stop his exits or to curb his insensitivities. She once told a friend, "I love him, but I don't like him."

As she got older, the constant pain forced her to abandon her career as a concert musician. So Carol took on the cause of people with disabilities. She showed courage in what she said and she had great empathy. But even then, the habits of denial and secrecy kept her from being genuine—or honest. Anne was astonished when she read this in one of the journal entries her mother wrote toward the end of her life: "But it was there and fortunately it was acknowledged and talked about among all of us that Mother was different." That was a lie.

Anne was appalled. "How could she possibly say this?" Anne realized "how her denial and false persona colored her own reality." It filled Anne with sadness, not only for her own solitary childhood "but for my mother as well, for surely her comments reflected her own yearnings, her own desires that she could talk to those she loved about her experience of spending most of her life unable to walk."

Anne was relieved finally to get to know the woman who raised her. Even though she wishes they had been able to connect while her mother was alive, Anne discovered that her mother was a real person, with fears and anger, love and pain. The diaries accomplished that. When Anne encountered her mother's authentic self, she suddenly found a hero—her mother.

Returning to Warm Springs, long after her own mother's death, Carol had had an epiphany that helped her understand what she had suffered. It enabled her daughter, many years later, to love her mother.

All of us belong to the human race.

All of us.

But we—I—endanger ourselves if we try to deny our truths, if we choose to ignore or repress our reality.

For then we lose part of ourselves and we have no chance of ever being whole.

Anne read, in her mother's words, the truth of Carol's desire for wholeness, something she was denied in childhood and something she could never share with Anne. Three generations were damaged by silence: Anne's grandfather never achieved the kind of intimacy and love he wanted to have with his daughter. Anne's mother yearned for a close family, which was impossible in their state of denial. Anne, in the face of her mother's silence, felt a terrible distance from her mother.

Polio is a virus. It is not genetic and cannot travel across generations. But silence in the face of tragedy is a burden borne by families throughout the years.

GETTING TO KNOW YOU

*The marriage of honesty
and intimacy*

Intimacy. That's what lies at the heart of close relationships. Intimacy is not easy to achieve, and there are lots of people who don't care for it. They don't want to be too close, too revealing, too, well, intimate. Intimacy requires an amalgam of honesty and trust. There are plenty of people who don't have the time and the emotional energy to get that close to others. Good friendships and family relationships can still flourish without the kind of intimacy I have been describing.

But there are certain kinds of relationships that require intimacy, and secrets do not foster it. Secrets close doors between people. The secret keeper has to skirt important subjects and becomes silent when the conversation gets too close. Meanwhile, the other person lives in a state of ignorance. You can't know what you don't know. All you can do is sense—if you are very alert—that something is awry.

The secret keeper trying to keep his stories straight in the company of close relatives and friends may feel like a short-order cook. Bacon and eggs for grandma, oatmeal for auntie, and coffee and Danish for the best friend. The secret keeper must present the correct version of himself or herself in every different aspect of life. It's hard work, managing this fragmentation, and over time the eggs, the cereal, and the coffee arrive at the table a little bit cool.

As we have seen, coming out with the truth is hard, just as hard—and often as painful—as learning the secret. This is a chapter about the return to intimacy, how it sometimes happens in unexpected ways, how people who can't find the truth suffer the loss of intimacy, and what it feels like to pay the price of honesty and reap its spiritual benefits.

This chapter looks at the issue in three ways. In the first story a woman who had a complicated and unsatisfactory relationship with her mother finds herself, much like Anne in the last chapter, feeling empathy and love when she comes upon the diaries her mother kept every day of her adult life. In the second, a young man discovers his father's secret life but never gets enough information from his father to understand the man. He suffers from the ambiguity all his life. And finally, a woman who is petrified to tell the truth about her experiences as a child, the secrets she held for others, and the truth about herself, gradually opens up and turns into the person she was meant to be.

Michelle Meets Her Mother

Michelle grew up in a troubled family. Nobody got along. Her parents fought and her father would drive off into the night when he couldn't take the yelling and screaming. He wouldn't come home until the next morning. Then Michelle's eldest sister died in childbirth, leaving her mother to care for the newborn grandchild while mourning her first daughter. Her mother was accomplished in many areas, but Michelle often felt as if her mother was a missing person, even if she didn't drive off into the night as her father did. Her mother was energetic in public and isolated in private. Michelle couldn't pin her down. But she knew that the difficult marriage was at the heart of her mother's misery. She just didn't know why.

Michelle remembers vividly the "day that everything changed, but nothing changed." She and her mother were in the kitchen when her dad called. Her parents spoke for a moment.

"You're telling me this now?"

Her voice was breaking and Michelle could hear the emotion as her mother's voice became shrill.

"You're telling me this now? Well what do you want me to do about it?" Her mother was sobbing.

"You hang up that phone and get home right now," her mother shouted as she slammed down the phone. Then she rested her head on her arms and wept.

Michelle had no idea what the news was, but her mother asked her to spend the rest of the weekend with a friend who lived nearby. In the ensuing years, her mother confided her sadness to Michelle but not its cause. When Michelle had her first child, her mother showed no interest in the baby. She wouldn't visit, much less provide the support Michelle needed in those scary early days of motherhood.

Her mom had a way of engaging and then disappearing. She was a brilliant artist and athlete—the perfect Northern California woman—who mastered many disciplines. But she had a problem with closeness. It often happened that just as she would get close to a friend or a colleague, she would break off the relationship. It was painful to watch and hard to understand. Over time, Michelle's mother developed bone cancer, which slowly and painfully killed her. It was a cruel disease, and her mother suffered every day until her death.

At her mother's funeral, Michelle's eulogy included a catalogue of her mother's accomplishments and a confession of her own ignorance.

"She taught art. She was in art shows. She taught music. She started in the backyard and then became a master gardener. She taught macramé, and then went to her shows. Then my mom wanted to be a teacher, but in the middle of it she studied transcendental meditation with the Maharishi Mahesh Yogi. Then my mom became a champion bridge player and bred wheaten terriers. She got her college degree when I was in high school, got her master's when I was in college, got her PhD when I was out of college. She wrote a book about poetry. Then got another master's in creative nonfiction, and then became a practicing Buddhist.

"You Buddhists didn't know my mother wrote a book, did you?

"You artists didn't know my mother was into marathon running. That she lifted weights and cooked. She was a Renaissance woman." Putting together all the disparate parts of her mother's life, Michelle concluded, "None of you knew my mother. I didn't know my mother." That was the sad truth.

Michelle felt a great sense of relief after the funeral because the burden of her mother's painful and prolonged suffering was lifted from her shoulders. But she didn't have much time to recover because a few days after the funeral, Michelle got an urgent phone call from her aunt. Her father had fainted and was at the hospital, but he refused to be admitted. Michelle sighed and headed to the hospital to meet him.

Her father insisted that he needed to get back to the house, *now*. He was adamant. But so was Michelle, who knew that he needed to be in the hospital. Her father eventually agreed to return to be admitted for observation, but only after he had gone home. So reluctantly Michelle took him to the house. He went in, picked up a backpack in the hall, shoved it into a closet, shut the door, and got back into the car. Once he was in his hospital bed, her father wanted to keep his wallet in the drawer, but it wasn't a safe thing to do, so after some acrimony, he tossed it to Michelle, who took her leave.

Early the next morning her father called. He needed the list of prescriptions from the wallet. So Michelle dumped all the cards and papers and found the list of medications and read them to the nurse. Then as she was stuffing all the bits back into her father's wallet, she noticed a slip of paper in his distinctive handwriting. On it were names of people and website addresses. Michelle was curious, so she went to the computer. The websites were gay porn. Michelle found other evidence of her father's sexuality in the wallet. Now she understood the long-distance phone call she had witnessed so many years ago. Her father had been telling her mother that he was gay. She also figured out what was in the backpack her father so urgently needed to hide—gay sex films.

At that point Michelle called her therapist. She chose the person who had helped her whole family through the death of her elder sister, a therapist who knew the family well. The therapist offered a warning: If Michelle brought this subject up with her father, it might increase the intimacy between them. Did Michelle really want that? She needed to think about it.

Michelle made no comment when she returned the wallet to her father and drove him home. She didn't raise the subject of what she had found. She and her father never got along, and she didn't care to get any closer to him. Making this choice, Michelle was also exiting her relationship with her father. Exhausted by the drama of her parents, she let him go.

Michelle's therapist gave her an important insight. If you want to keep your distance, let the secret you have discovered pass unmentioned. Don't raise the subject; don't ask any questions. Let it go. Let the relationship slide. Some relationships merit that decision. So that was the end of the emotional connection with her father, which had always been a troubled and hurtful one. Michelle was relieved. But her mother, whom she loved and still longed for, even though she was dead, remained an enigma.

Some months after this incident, her father called to say that he had sold the house and was moving into a condo. Did she want her mother's books? They were packed in cartons and ready to go. She could take them or they would be donated or thrown out. Of course Michelle wanted them. So she packed the boxes in her car, took them home, and piled them in her basement. A few weeks later, she went through the cartons. "I cut the first one open, start sorting them, books about Buddhism will go to the Buddhist people, books about writing, maybe I'll give to my novelist friend. Books about poetry I'm going to keep." Michelle was gradually getting through this trove of books and then "I hit the box with thirty years of my mother's journals. And I'm like, oh my God, it's the mother lode."

This is how Michelle met her mother. She already understood why her mother was weeping at the kitchen table all those years ago, but she didn't know what she'd lived through afterward. Her mother longed for the intimacy of a real marriage, and she was unutterably lonely. One journal entry recounts a conversation between her parents. Her mother said, "I wish I was a man so that you would love me. You know I just wish you loved me for who I am." And her father said, "I love you as much as I could ever love anyone." Her mother then confided to her diary: "I can't imagine loving someone as much as I love him, but I wish I were a boy."

As Michelle began to see what her mother had been up against, she could empathize with her mother's sadness and loneliness. Now she could understand her mother's need to keep in constant motion. Her misery fueled the restless energy for all her accomplishments. And her sense of diminishment pushed her to perpetually strive to reach new and different heights.

As Michelle continued to read the journals, she discovered a deeper source of her mother's misery. It took her mother years of journaling to sketch out her secret, to write the truth, and then to face it. The truth made her dad's betrayal seem minor to Michelle. The diary opens up gradually.

"So the first ten years of these journals that I dive into, my mother is exploring that she has some unpleasant feelings about her father." Michelle's grandfather came for dinner every Sunday night. She always thought of her grandfather as a handsome gentleman in a shaggy fisherman's sweater, standing around at the magnificent farmer's market, talking with the suppliers and flirting with the shoppers. "He was a well-read and charming gentleman."

Ten years into the diary, her mother wrote, "My father was inappropriate with me." In the second decade of her journals her mother admitted, "I was fondled by my father." In the last decade she says, "My father came to my bedroom on the night of my wedding ceremony and said you won't be my little girl anymore." Michelle believes that "fondle" is the polite way to refer to all inappropriate sexual behavior with a child. She pointed out that the Penn State sex scandal was first reported as "fondling" when the truth was that the coach was raping little boys.

Michelle was shocked and heartbroken. She loved her grandfather, who had been a constant presence in her life. This revelation brought her into a different level of contact with her mother. But Michelle needed confirmation. It was too shocking to accept on the basis of the diary. Maybe her mother was making things up. So Michelle went to her uncle, who was her mother's twin brother. Although he and Michelle's mother had stopped seeing each other years ago, Michelle had kept up a warm relationship with him and his wife. She visited them in Florida the Thanksgiving after her mother's death, arriving a day early so she could start to cook in the morning. After she arrived, Michelle made a cup of tea and sat on the balcony overlooking the ocean with her aunt and uncle. She jumped right in.

"I read my mom's journals. I saw how profoundly damaged she was psychologically by the abuse that took place in her home." Her uncle nodded. He recalled dinners with their parents. Their father would quiz him about school and current affairs and history. Michelle read aloud what her mother had written about the same events: "After they had finished talking, I was invited to sit on my father's lap. I learned about sex, I learned what sexy was from my father."

Her uncle recalled how much he resented the fact that he was being quizzed about things intellectual while his twin sister was getting all the loving. Michelle replied that her mother was jealous of the intellectual attention her twin received at the dinner table. Wasn't she worthy of that kind of attention? she had asked in her journals. Why was she only good for the sexy stuff?

Michelle had found some photographs of her teenage mother posed in her bra and underwear. She mentioned the pictures to her uncle. He was quiet, and then his voice filled with emotion.

"Well, you know who took those pictures, don't you?"

"Your father."

"Yes."

"You're telling me it stopped with the bra and underwear?" Michelle paused, waiting for a definitive response that never came.

"I don't know, maybe it did, maybe it didn't. I'm telling you that it was wrong."

Then Michelle looked straight at her beloved uncle.

"I think about what the effect was on you." Her uncle was silent. "You have been carrying around shame about your sister, anger toward your father, disappointment in your mother."

That was enough for one evening, so they bade each other good night and went to bed. The next morning, as Michelle started to cook Thanksgiving dinner, her aunt and uncle appeared. They came in separately.

"It was so helpful for you to talk to us about that abuse," they each said. "We never really thought about how much of an influence that had."

Over time more of her mother's behavior became clear to Michelle. She remembers, "My mother flirted with all my boyfriends. She maintained correspondence with my ex-boyfriends, and no boundaries, no boundaries." Michelle understands why now. "As soon as you're violated by your father or your mother, or by an adult in charge, right and wrong are gone. It's all gray."

The disappointment and anger began to fade as Michelle learned about her mother's childhood. "It was not until I read the journal and I saw in her words her struggle to come to terms with it, and I saw that photograph of her in her bra and underwear, that it became real. It's gotten below the intellectual level for me. I'm no longer just intellectualizing it. I'm having empathy for my mother."

Even though her mother is dead, and even though her relationship with her father has ended, Michelle no longer feels isolated from her parents. "I spent all these years in therapy trying to undo the 'what's wrong with me' thing, until I realized that what was wrong was that my mother was incapable of forming those connections."

Reconciliation for Michelle was one-sided. She couldn't let her mother know how much she now understood and how much more she admired this driven and gifted woman. But for Michelle, resolution nonetheless followed upon revelation.

Papers in the Attic

Throughout the history of theater, from *Oedipus Rex* to Jon Robin Baitz's *Other Desert Cities*, the revelation of a secret is the denouement of the action. A young man learns he has been sleeping with his mother and puts out his eyes. The play is over. The angry daughter learns her parents' secret, then the curtain falls. Unfortunately—or happily—real life offers a fourth act. If after the telling there is silence, or another cover-up, then the secret continues to do harm. We have seen how resolution so often depends on the story that follows the first revelation.

But sometimes we cannot get the whole story, and even worse, we may get two conflicting ones. That creates stasis: Did it happen this way, or that way? Was my father a terrible man, or not? It is hard to survive in such limbo, which is where Eugene has landed. He must hold two contradictory versions of the truth at the same time and cannot solve the puzzle. His uncertainty is a misery.

Eugene has carried his burden for most of his sixty years. Look into his brooding eyes and you see sorrow, even when he is laughing. His story begins when he was fifteen. A little detective, Eugene was always checking out hiding places. He found his parents' love letters hidden in his mother's sewing room (he thought they were disgusting), and he found his father's condoms hidden in a box in his bathroom (he didn't know what they were exactly, but he knew enough to exit the bathroom pronto). Eugene grew up in one of those great old Victorian houses. The attic consisted of a warren of tiny rooms piled high with cartons and packages, papers and castoffs. Now the family was leaving this house to move to another city, and the attic was in the process of being cleaned out. What a gold mine for a curious teenager.

One afternoon he came across a carton of thirty-year-old newspapers from World War II. They were quite a find for this future historian, and he pawed through them with delight. Then something caught his eye: His father's name appeared on the front page of the paper, and so did Eugene's. But Eugene was not born until after the war.

The article told the story of a prominent physician, Eugene's father, and his wife, the mother of twins, a girl and a boy (named Eugene), who were divorcing. The wife, a Frenchwoman, the article said, had abandoned her husband and taken her children to North Africa, where she was living with a German general and having a fine old time in the barracks.

It is not uncommon for men to hide their first marriages and children from their second family. I have heard many such stories. They want to make a fresh start, and they don't want to have to come up with awkward explanations. Usually the second wife is aware of the situation, but the kids are kept in the dark. Eugene was shocked and scared, unnerved at the thought that somebody else carried his name and was his father's son. "I couldn't believe it. I put it back, and I walked down the staircase to the second floor just feeling absolutely sick, and I went and lay on my bed."

The newspaper carried a date in the early 1940s. Eugene knew that the Nazis had overrun France in 1940 and many people had fled to safety elsewhere. He knew his father carried dual French and American citizenship. Were these people his relatives? Why didn't he know about them? Why did his father lie, and what did his mother know? Eugene didn't have the courage to confront his distant and formal parents with his discovery. "It just didn't make any sense to me. I couldn't understand this. I wandered around for a few days. I didn't ask my parents about it. But I remember looking at my father and thinking he was the biggest liar I'd ever known."

Luckily, that weekend an old friend of his father's dropped by, and Eugene ran to the car. He asked him what he knew of the story in the paper. "I remember, he put his hands on my face, very warmly." He looked at Eugene and said, "I think you'd better talk to your father." So Eugene knew that it was true. He asked this friend to be his messenger, to tell his father what he had discovered, and to say that Eugene wanted to talk. Nothing happened. Then one afternoon, a grim-looking father appeared in Eugene's room.

"Would you like to take a train ride this weekend?" Eugene nodded. His father loved trains, especially the historic train that went north for two hours and then returned home. "I remember when he put on the tweed overcoat, and a touring cap, and a camera around his neck. He always dressed that way when we were traveling, and I was horribly embarrassed because he looked like a tourist."

They didn't speak for the first two hours. As they started the journey home, his father finally turned to Eugene and said, "I think you have some questions for me, what are your questions?"

Eugene asked, "Who are these people?"

"How do you know about that?"

Eugene told him how he'd found the old newspaper.

And so his father launched into the story of his first wife, his children, and his divorce and subsequent marriage to Eugene's mother. In the 1930s Eugene's father, who was practicing medicine in France, had fallen in love and married a woman who came from a French military family. They had twins, a girl and a boy. As the German invasion loomed, Eugene's father, who by this time had established himself in America as well as in France, decided to take his family to the United States.

He told Eugene he had acquired passage to New York for the whole family and set a time for them all to meet at the wharf before the ship left. His wife and children never appeared, so he departed without them, not knowing what had kept them away. By this time the marriage was rocky, so Eugene's father assumed she didn't want to accompany him, even though America meant safety for her and the twins. After that, all his father knew were rumors. He believed that she had attached herself to a German general and that she was sleeping her way across North Africa.

"I asked him a lot of questions. I remember he cried. I had never seen my father cry before, ever. And I cried, too."

The train trip was almost over, and so was the conversation. His father said, "I will never speak to you about this again. Don't ever ask me about this."

When they got home, Eugene went to his mother.

"Is this true?" he asked her.

"I can't speak to you about it," she said.

Eugene returned to the attic in search of more newspapers. All the cartons had been removed.

His father's story had so many holes in it, and Eugene had no way to fill them in. Why didn't his father go looking for his wife and children? Eugene knew that France on the eve of the German invasion was chaotic, but surely there were relatives and friends who could have helped him find his family. The notion of his father simply going to his cabin in the ship and making the voyage to America alone was painful to hear and hard to fathom. If it were true as told, then what kind of a man was his father not to try to find his family? And if it weren't true, how could Eugene discover the facts? What he took from his father and mother that day was a sense that their past was off-limits, a closed book.

"I'll never discuss it with you again," in this context, is one of the cruelest expressions in the English language. Eugene was left with a pile of questions, none of which would be answered. So he struggled to come to terms with the story. He had to face the fact that his father was a liar; otherwise the first family would not have been kept secret. How could Eugene love a man who would leave his children and wife to the Nazis? Why didn't he look for them after the war? Even if he had been devastated by his wife's behavior, surely he had some feelings for his children. Eugene had always found his father cold and distant. But this story seemed beyond comprehension. Who was this man?

Eugene could imagine the terrible pain his father might have felt, being abandoned by his family and learning that his wife had been unfaithful. That might explain some of his behavior, but as Eugene grew up, he came to believe that blaming a woman's morals is a common way to undermine her. That version of the story didn't sit well with a young man who had a powerful sense of fairness and justice. What about his mother, who refused to talk? Did she know about the first family? If she did, how could she have married his father? Did she believe the woman abandoned his father at the dock? Eugene's mother was not gullible. She was a smart and subtle woman.

The puzzle remained. Then, some eight years later, Eugene's father passed away. The French take citizenship very seriously, and the government made sure that all his father's children were informed, including the first wife and the twins, who were now in their forties. A few weeks later, a letter arrived. It was from his brother, the first Eugene, who called himself by his middle name, François. He had been informed of his father's death and had tracked down Eugene's mother. Now a second version of the story emerged.

When they met, François explained that his parents' marriage was falling apart in the late 1930s. He told Eugene "my father abandoned them, that he had long wanted to get rid of his wife, he hated her." On the eve of the German invasion, his father headed off alone on a ship bound for the United States. The children were collateral damage. François's mother, the daughter of an old French military family, fled south, as did many French people (the history books and novels of the time are full of such stories). She arrived in North Africa, where she lived under the protection of the Vichy authorities. She never took up with a German officer, as that newspaper said (Eugene believes the reporter was fed this story by his father or one of his close associates), and she struggled to raise the twins in North Africa until the war was over. Then they returned to Paris, where their mother's family, who took to calling Eugene's father "the beast," cared for them. A civil divorce did take place, which the first wife, a strict Catholic, never accepted. Two years later Eugene's father remarried and started his second family. His first wife considered him a bigamist. But there is more to the story.

Eugene learned that his own mother played a role in the life of the French family. "She knew about these children, and even had an address." After the war, his mother secretly "sent them things. She sent them boxes of food, she sent them photographs." François remembers this and is grateful. When François went back to France, Eugene discussed this with his mother. She admitted her role in helping her husband's first family. "She said she would post the letters herself, post the packages herself without his knowing." These letters and the gifts made it possible for the three of them to survive that terrible winter of 1946 and the year that followed. Food was scarce. People froze and starved all over Europe. Eugene tells me that François "still talks about this, my mother's kindness."

As his mother opened up, Eugene learned another piece of the story. During the war, his mother and father attempted to get the twins away from their mother in North Africa and bring them to safety in America. They used their contacts in the State Department and spent time and money trying to make this happen. It didn't work. As French citizens, the twins couldn't be shuttled across the Atlantic at the whim of their absent father.

In this moment of confession, Eugene's mother told him another story. This one happened in the 1950s. She and his father had gone to France with his two sisters and were taking delight in the pleasures of Paris. Suddenly Eugene's half brother appeared at the hotel where they were staying, hoping to see his father. His mother told how she and Eugene's sisters spent the day with him, her heart breaking all the while. "My father would have nothing to do with him, left the hotel, went God knows where for the entire day, left my mother with this boy, this twenty-year-old boy." When Eugene reminded his sisters about this incident, they were pleased to know the identity of the lovely young man who had spent the day with them in Paris. They had no idea who he was. Eugene's half brother looks just like him, with the same wide forehead and brooding eyes. He adores Eugene's mother and will forever be grateful for her generosity. Eugene is bemused because his mother always seemed a difficult woman to him, demanding, cold, and harsh. He had to revise his thinking when he learned of her secret kindness to her husband's first family.

So his mother comes off better than he could ever imagine, and his brother is a lovely man. But whose story is right? Both Eugene's father and his first wife are dead, and they took the truth to their graves. François, now seventy-five, asks himself every day how his father could have done these terrible things to him and his family.

Eugene doesn't know for sure. But François's story makes sense. Marriage on the rocks, children and wife abandoned but secure in a military family. And so do the actions of Eugene's mother. She empathized with the plight of her husband's first family. Eugene's mother came from a culture of noblesse oblige, and charity to the children would have been second nature. So would secrecy. Her unforgiving husband would have put a stop to it, had he known. Eugene has not brought up the subject in years. "She's ninety-six years old, and she's a very intelligent woman, and if she started to lie awake and think about this, it could shatter something."

Where does that leave Eugene? He has come to appreciate his mother's kindness to the French family. She was a cold and strict mother with her own children, and this compassion opened a well of affection for her in Eugene's heart. But the ambiguity of his family history was impossible for him to bear. So he has come to a conclusion about his father. "In fact, my father should never have been a father, he wasn't a good one." He wasn't a good one to his first family, and he was not a good father to his second family. That Eugene knows. He has chosen to adopt a terrible truth about his father in the place of ambiguity. It isn't pleasant for him, but he accepts it.

In choosing to accept the more difficult truth about his father, Eugene has taken up the task his father never shouldered—to be a faithful and loving husband and father to his own wife and two daughters. Accepting his father has strengthened his resolve to be a better person. This may be his father's lasting legacy—Eugene is the reverse of him. As for his mother, Eugene discovered a woman he never knew. It would have been beyond Eugene's imagination to think of his straitlaced mother sending money and food packages to her husband's former family. He could not fathom his mother lying to her husband and going behind his back. So the sorrow of recognizing the truth of his father is mitigated by the warmth of discovering his mother's depths.

Stories about hidden first families like Eugene's abounded in the postwar period. Later in the century, such stories were easier to tell and to learn. So it has been with sexuality. It isn't so long ago that most gay people were ashamed to come out of the closet to their families. Things are getting better, but we need to remember the past. It offers a historical perspective on many different kinds of secrets.

I have a friend whose brother came out to their parents when he was nearly thirty. The mother was heartbroken. Because her son was gay? Not at all. She was devastated that he thought she would reject him because of his sexuality. It broke her heart that he didn't trust her enough to tell her his secret.

Things don't always happen that way. Families can break up when a child comes out. Parents divorce when the secret of an affair is revealed. People stop speaking to each other when a humiliating flaw or a terrible set of actions is revealed. So the person with a secret is constantly forced to make cost-benefit calculations about the price of telling the truth.

Jackie did this for most of her life. She knew the truth would cost her dearly. For many years she drank heavily to deal with her pain. But then she sobered up and took to heart the famous Alcoholics Anonymous adage: You are only as sick as your secrets. So she began her long journey to truthfulness. She risked everything. Her family did not welcome the truth. Nobody patted her on the back when she finally told her parents why she couldn't get along with her brother. The Catholic Church wasn't interested in her deep faith. In each instance, Jackie paid a price. She was criticized, threatened, exiled. But she didn't stop her search for wholeness. When she eventually found it, she reconnected with the parts of her life from which she felt she had been excommunicated.

Jackie Takes Risks

Jackie was four when she realized she was different. "My kindergarten teacher, Miss Carol, was gorgeous. I immediately fell in love with her. I knew I had feelings that were unusual." As she got older, Jackie wanted to be a boy because she got crushes on girls and thought that's what boys did. She liked the way boys dressed, and she couldn't stand frills. There were two girls on the block where Jackie grew up, Glenda and Diane, and they dressed up in their mommies' clothes, which is what all the girls did. Jackie couldn't: "I wasn't going to ever do it." And then, because she wanted to be friends with them, she made the attempt. She remembers the day when she thought, "I'm going to really try. I'm going to really, really try." So Jackie dressed in some of her mother's clothes and went to the back door to meet her friends outside. But she couldn't get through the door. "I just cried and cried."

Jackie had been a fervent Catholic from an early age, and she participated in church activities whenever she could. She knew the liturgy by heart. So after this incident Jackie decided to say mass in the dining room. She would wear a robe she had found in the attic and drape one of her father's ties across her shoulders. A goblet became the chalice. Jackie put flying-saucer candies in a dish—they were the wafers. "I was a pious kid. I really wanted to have a direct line to God." She couldn't tell anyone about her odd affections and desires. They must be evil. So she kept them secret.

Jackie's second reason for her belief that she was in serious need of God's grace came from her older brother. He was a bully who never cared for his little sister and was perpetually mean. He would tear her down verbally and occasionally hit her. By the time Jackie was eight, her brother and his best friend, who were eleven years old, started to take her down to the basement. Her brother's friend would undress Jackie and play with her. Her brother played a secondary role in this, but he never tried to stop the sexual games. "It happened a number of times." This sent the terrible message to Jackie that "All I was good for was sex." That was another secret she couldn't tell. First of all, she believed it was her fault; second, she thought her brother would kill her if she told. She also knew her parents would blame her. They could never see their troubled son for who he was, not then and not now.

Wanting to be normal, and thinking that marriage might cure her, she married a nice guy right after high school. It never worked. She had girlfriends over when her policeman husband was on night duty, and they played around. She was miserable about it, but she couldn't stop. "So those secrets were probably the most destructive for me because even though I had trouble in my marriage, I loved my husband. I didn't want to hurt him." Worse than that: "I didn't want to be who I was."

During this time, she and her husband lived in the same apartment building as her brother and his first wife, and Jackie saw what was happening between them. There was terrible physical abuse, and her brother's wife didn't want Jackie to tell her parents. Jackie had to keep another secret, this one for her sister-in-law. "Ultimately I was the one who whisked her away and got her out of the marriage." She couldn't tell anybody, but for Jackie that secret felt good. "There's always the part of feeling powerful because you're the confidante. That you are the person they trust and feel safe with, and that always feels very good."

Jackie eventually divorced her husband. Their marriage wasn't fair to him—or to her. She never confided the reason to him, and to this day she feels terrible about it. "It was brutal. Having to betray my own values to survive is what was so excruciatingly painful." After the divorce was final, Jackie began to breathe easier. She was more comfortable in her own skin and began to become acquainted with the truth. "I had no stomach for lying. It's like I couldn't do it anymore. It wasn't my nature."

But her family's view of life and the truth of her sexuality were in deep conflict. Having a gay daughter was out of the question, a humiliation not to be borne. The culture of these Slovakian immigrants was not accepting. If shame is a major source of secrecy, the probable loss of love is also a major deterrent to the truth. So Jackie struggled.

At this point in her life, there was only one route for Jackie to take: away from her family. But she couldn't sustain the distance for long. This state of being in geographic exile was hard for her, and eventually she decided to come out to her mother. She just had to. She knew there wouldn't be applause and hugs, but she was prepared. She went to her parents' home. Jackie sat at the kitchen table while her mother was cutting up vegetables. She chopped methodically.

"What's the matter?" her mother said. "You seem sad."

"I am sad, Mom."

"Boy problems?"

"Mom, you know I don't have a boyfriend."

Silence. Chop, chop, chop.

"I have girl problems."

The chopping stopped. Her mother didn't turn around. She was facing the wall. Jackie was on the other side of the kitchen.

"Don't tell your father," her mother said. She was still facing the wall, and resumed chopping.

Now Jackie was relieved of her secret, but her mother wanted her to keep the truth from her father. By this time Jackie was fed up with keeping secrets—and her father already knew, even though she'd never had to spell it out the way she did in the kitchen. Jackie remembers the time the subject first came up with him. Jackie was in love with someone but wasn't sure it made sense to move in with her.

"Dad," she said, "I don't know what I should do, I really want to move in with this woman Carol." Her father asked for the pros and cons.

Finally, he said, "Do you love her?"

"Yeah, I do, Dad, I love her a lot."

"Then do it. If it's not right, it won't work out and you'll leave."

That was Jackie's father. "He didn't care, he just loved me."

Not so her brother, who was enraged when he learned of Jackie's sexuality. He couldn't stand it. They had been at odds for years. Jackie had refused to attend his second wedding. Her parents were furious at her decision not to go, and they got into a fight about it. In desperation Jackie revealed what had taken place in the basement all those years ago. Her parents were upset, but they went to the wedding and didn't say a word to their son. Then he and his wife had a little girl. At the christening, Jackie's mother pulled Jackie's brother into the corner and told him she knew about what he and his friend had done to Jackie in the basement. Jackie thought this was wrong. "You don't do that to a person at his child's christening." He was ripping mad. A year later, Jackie accompanied her mother to visit her brother's wife and baby. Her brother turned up. He had a hammer in one hand, and he was in a rage. He started yelling and screaming at the top of his lungs and shaking the hammer in her face.

"What the fuck are you saying?" her brother shouted. "I never did anything like that." Then he took a breath. "I never screwed you, and to me, that would be sexual abuse."

Jackie grabbed her mother and got into the car. He was right. That didn't happen, but plenty of other stuff did. Jackie and her brother did not speak for the next nine years, and he kept her away from her nieces. She paid a steep price for telling this secret.

Jackie's other home was the parish church. Catholicism was central to her life, but when she joined the lesbian community in downtown New York, she had to leave the church. She was not welcome there. Her desire to be close to God was deep, but the church closed its doors to her.

After her father died, Jackie was left with a mother who was ashamed of her, a furious alcoholic brother, and a church that disapproved of her. She built a life in the 1970s and '80s in the East Village, where her talents and energy made her a star.

But she was drinking and she was sad. She knew that alcohol, which was her brother's drug of choice, was doing her no good. She needed to get well. Alcoholics Anonymous was her salvation. The twelve steps were her path to authenticity. She found a wise and caring sponsor, and she began to get a glimmer of her own wisdom and strength.

Resilience started to show itself in Jackie's life. She accepted her family for their prejudices and anger, but she wouldn't give them up. She even talked her brother into helping her renovate her mother's house, so that Jackie could live upstairs and care for her mother as she got older. Brother and sister were able to work side by side. There was a moment when her brother came the closest he ever could to an apology. He said, "I guess I was never really there for you." Jackie just nodded: "I held my tongue because I wanted to say, 'And you still aren't.'" After the renovation was complete, Jackie moved in with her mother.

They got along all right, but there was conflict. Her mother still disapproved of Jackie's sexuality. It was a big issue between them. Jackie wasn't happy, but she stuck with it. She didn't see a choice. "And then you go and you spend time with the family. It's very complex because the stronger you become who you actually are, the more you want to just be who you are with them."

Then, at an AA dance, Jackie met the love of her life. When they decided to marry, their friends were thrilled, but not her family. Neither her mother nor her brother attended the wedding. Then Jackie brought her wife home to live in the house she shared with her mother. Gradually Jackie's mother came to love her wife. The tradition of building and improving in Jackie's life continued as she found a way to make peace with her brother. She realized that the two people who mattered most to him were his daughters, and so she started sending them gifts to help them with their education. Things got better. Jackie and her wife celebrated their first wedding anniversary with her brother at his home.

The only door that remained slammed shut was the church. And then something miraculous happened. Jackie discovered an underground branch of the church that was reading scripture along the lines of Vatican II, which was liberal and accepted gays. To be able to attend mass in a welcoming environment was a crowning event for Jackie. Last year, she attended a meeting of gay Catholics. "I saw these people talk about secrets, oh, they're in such incredible pain because they can't resolve being gay and being Catholic. And they don't see who they really are."

Jackie has found that being of service to others is her true vocation. It begins at home. She has started taking her mother to mass. "The hill is too steep for her now. She can't walk it. So she wasn't going to mass for a long time." Jackie didn't care for the church near them, and then she found one she liked. "So this is a new thing I do with my mom. I go to mass with my mother on Sundays."

Jackie always knew she was different, and she experienced how those differences aroused anger, rejection, and judgment. Even in this hostile environment, she felt that protecting herself by keeping secrets was a betrayal of her truthfulness and integrity. Finding her own truth ended her need for secrets. She found that being truthful could make her whole.

"I'm an integrated person. I'm the same with my mother as I am with my friends as I am with you. I'm the same everywhere. That is such a blessing because that's what I missed in my life for a long time because everything had to be compartmentalized for me to manage it."

Managing a secret is work. The Keeper stays alert, knowing that different surroundings require different personalities. It's a full-time job, which Michelle's mother played all her life. Eugene's parents did the same, and so did Jackie for a long time. Truth brings a sigh of relief—even though it is hard to bear and unpleasant to think about, and miserable to consider revealing. No more putting on a false front to the rest of the world. No more building little fences around yourself. Sometimes we pay the price of truth when we look into the eyes of people we have disappointed. But we always imagined their disappointment— or we would not have kept our secret from the outset.

And the people who count in our lives, the ones from whom we keep our secrets and to whom we reveal them, also have a choice. They may be dumbfounded at the truth and hurt by the loss of trust. They can turn from us in disgust, never to appear again. But days follow upon days, and so do weeks, and months, and years. Some revelations stop relationships in their tracks. But others reveal the true person in our midst, the imperfect, limping, and often loving soul we cared about so much. And so we continue to care, and together we can rebuild, this time slowly, on a foundation of truth. We can build a house together, or a home, or a beautiful garden that is nourished by acceptance.

We have choices in this life, and we make mistakes. Forgiveness is not impossible, and the wholeness of spirit that comes from truth is cool and pure.

EPILOGUE: AT LEAST I KNOW

Sharing sad truths makes
us stronger

My story continues from that New Year's Eve when Jonathan and I found each other again over roast beef and the music of Mozart. When I got home from Jonathan's that night, it was nearly three in the morning, but I picked up the phone and called him. "I love you," I said. He didn't respond in kind, but I could tell he was glad.

Our connection was rekindled. We fell back into the rhythms of closeness that had begun nearly thirty years earlier. In the beginning, I was more forthcoming and Jonathan was more cautious. He had been deeply hurt, and he didn't trust me. He kept saying, "You are Mary Poppins. When will the north wind blow you away?" I wasn't going anywhere, but it took time for him to believe it.

Then as I prepared to move out of the apartment Dick and I had shared, I came upon a blue jewelry box. I didn't recognize it. When I opened it, I nearly fainted. Here was the pin Jonathan's parents had given me. I had not touched the box in all those years. A few weeks later, I wore the pin to a wedding party.

When I took off my coat, Jonathan saw it and rocked back on his heels. "My father has good taste," he said.

So much of it was easy. I knew his parents from long ago, and they loved me. His best friend forgave me and his wife embraced us. But most important for me was the fact that I could tell Jonathan whatever I felt, happy or sad. I had vowed that I would try not to cover up my feelings. This time I would be real. If I was angry, I blew up. He responded in kind. If something made him sad or hurt his feelings, he let me know. Initially it was hard to be forthright and hard to hear his complaints. But soon I relaxed. It seemed that being honest didn't make us hate each other. It brought us closer. A few years later, we decided to get married.

Over the twenty years we were together, my sons and their families came to accept Jonathan. At first they were dubious. He had no children and was not inclined to share me, especially with my grown sons. When they visited us at the beach and spread out over the furniture, Jonathan referred to them as "the mammals."

I had spent so much energy trying to make sure that my sons were close to their father that I was tapped out when it came to fixing their relationship with Jonathan. He had bad habits, and they resented him. I was sorry but felt that now it was my turn. I had sacrificed plenty being their mother in my first marriage. Now I wanted to be a wife. The boys kept their distance, but this was a time when they were building their own lives, marriages, and careers. They were busy, too, I told myself.

Jonathan and I had a good time. We had grown up in the

same milieu. We liked the same books and disliked the same people. He had been a brilliant editor and was now an agent, so we had a shorthand language about book publishing. All his life and throughout his career, Jonathan loved women, and he loved talent, so talented women were his delight. His pride in my achievements could be read in his shining black eyes. When I decided to quit my last job, Jonathan got anxious. What would I do at home? I would miss the company and excitement. But that never happened. I enjoyed writing, and it was especially easy because I had him—my first and best reader.

He read so quickly that it seemed as if he inhaled the pages. I would give him a sheaf of pages to read. And then I would wait. If he read slowly, I needed to rewrite. When a section worked, he would flip the pages and look over at me with a smile. Thumbs up. It was ready to go. When I was disappointed and fussy, he would wrinkle his nose and say, "Is there an author in the room?" That brought me down to earth.

Over time, we spent afternoons with the Manhattan grandkids. Jonathan adored them and they loved him back. He tried to imbue them with a sense of humor. So he would say to Benji, "Two gorillas got on a bus . . ." The three-year-old would look at me to see if Pop Pop was serious. I would smile, and so would he. Things began to slow down a bit, Jonathan didn't want to go out much, but we had a relaxed, tender time together. It was going to last forever.

Then one weekend when I was out of town celebrating a cousin's birthday, Jonathan went to the doctor to have a blood test, following up on some puzzling results from his last physical. He called me to say that the hematologist wanted to do a bone marrow test, and that he had agreed to it—right then. Normally Jonathan was a fraidycat. He usually had to take a tranquilizer before going for a physical, so I was pleased that he'd been so efficient this time. I wasn't so happy to learn the results of the test: He had leukemia. But it was treatable. By the time we got to the doctor to discuss the diagnosis, Jonathan had deteriorated and was soon diagnosed with lymphoma, which had progressed so far that there was no treatment.

I took him home from the hospital to die. We both understood what was happening. The hospice bed was waiting in his room, and my youngest son was there, welcoming us home. It was hard for me to face Jonathan's imminent death. I wept in solitude. But what surprised me was that Jonathan took the bad news with sorrow yet equanimity. This man who fainted at the sight of blood said he thought this turn of events was bizarre, but he didn't deny the truth. Sometimes he tried to think himself into a state of hopefulness, but he soon returned to reality. Jonathan never lost his sense of humor. One day when we were fighting with hospice to get Jonathan the sleeping pills he needed, he stood up at his walker and yelled, "A dying man deserves his meds!" He got them. Jonathan felt bad about two things he knew he would miss: Benji's bar mitzvah and the Academy Awards.

I asked his friends and colleagues from his nearly fifty years in the book business to write him funny notes about the great times they had spent together. Some of the people who had hurt his feelings sent notes of love. His oldest friends came to say goodbye. They didn't weep until they left his room.

"This is the prequel," he said to me as he read the e-mails and thought about the visits. "I'm going to miss the main event." Jewish mystics believe that the spirit hangs around at least until the end of shivah, the seven days of mourning, so I told Jonathan that his spirit would be there for the funeral. We laughed.

We cried together, too, and we talked about the past with good feelings and the future with worry. It was very sad. I weep as I write this, years later. But it was good. Those hours we spent together in the last weeks and days were golden. I think of this as our time of honey, and I was storing it in the beehive of my memory.

As Jonathan began his passage to death, I kept on talking to him. I had been told that hearing is the last sense to go. Stories followed upon stories, and then I was out of words. So I decided to chronicle the Paris restaurants we had been to on our honeymoon. I got a smile when I mentioned the place we had to walk miles to find and a nod when I said I pardoned him for spending so much on a bottle of wine at Taillevent.

Now it was New Year's Eve. My eldest son had left his family on their holiday to be with me, and we had a good dinner, with champagne. I took my champagne glass to Jonathan and slipped a few spoonfuls into his mouth.

"Happy New Year," I said.

There was no response. He was slipping away. Then I said, "Show me you love me."

He opened his eyes, waved his fingers, and made a funny face. When his eyes closed, I wept.

He died the next evening. We had twenty-one years to the day. What I learned from this time was that a shared truth, as painful as it gets, gives you strength. The intimacy we shared in those last weeks was the best of our lives.

During those difficult days, I kept saying to myself, "At least I know." It became my mantra. I learned after Jonathan's death that when you face the truth together, you are on solid ground. If either or both of us had moved into denial, we never would have had that honey time together. I am grateful for those days and evenings.

Six months after his death, I went back to work on this book. I had learned something important: that even when things are terrible, if you face them together you can reach the very best in you. Accepting the truth gives you the strength to deal with whatever comes your way.

"At least I know." That sentence has carried me through rocky times since Jonathan's death. Facing the truth, however much you may dislike it, gives you power. It releases your strength, liberates your resilience, and calls forth your very human ability to put new and difficult events into perspective.

I don't mean to say that everybody should tell everyone every secret. But I think that facing the truth is not as bad as some people fear. And I have come to believe that the energy soaked up by denial can be put to more creative and loving use.

So please do not fear the truth, however much it may hurt. Healing comes in the morning. And life has a way of going on.

Acknowledgments

So many people have contributed to this book by telling me their stories. I thank you. Offering to be interviewed on this intimate and sometimes embarrassing subject takes courage. I hope I have done you justice.

My editors include the great Phyllis Grann, who wields the smartest pencil on the planet, and Kristine Puopolo, whose interest and encouragement mean so much. Mary Pipher is more than a reader. She is a mentor and a dear friend. I couldn't have done any of this without her. Celina Ottaway, journalist and novelist, taught me how to write a story and urged me not to turn away from the truth, even when it wasn't fun. Thank you.

Liz Darhansoff, first a neighbor, then a friend, and now an indispensable person in my life, has been where I needed her in the hard times, and now she is my agent. How lucky am I to have her in my life.

Tina Weiner, Naomi Meyer, and Alexandra Fahrni have, as always, listened to my stories beyond their patience. They have dealt with my concerns, worries, and joys as I worked during these years on the book. What good friends you are!

My children and grandchildren give me the energy to get out of bed in the morning and to face the keyboard—and the rest of my life. Special thanks to Benjamin, who at the age of seven suggested the title for the chapter on silence, "If You See Something, Say Something."

I began this book when my husband was still alive. He thought it was a splendid subject for me, and when I flagged, because it is so complex and sad, he urged me on. Without his encouragement, I would not have persevered. And what I learned from his death has permeated my thinking about the power of truth.

A Note on Sources

I grew up in a Freudian home, and psychological thinking has permeated my life—for good or ill. But in recent decades, scientific findings in neuroscience, psychology, and evolutionary theory have enriched our thinking about what it is to be human. The emergence of emotion and irrationality as full-fledged attributes of *Homo sapiens* makes it much easier to understand the dynamics of behavior described in this book.

Antonio Damasio, in *Descartes' Error* and subsequent books, has demonstrated the powerful role of emotion in our decision-making. His description of the autobiographical self, created by narratives that occur instantaneously in the unconscious and regularly in our consciousness, helped me to understand why we are so rocked by revelations that change our past before our eyes.

Carol Tavris and Elliot Aronson, in their brilliant book *Mistakes Were Made (But Not by Me)*, give life and texture to the discovery of cognitive dissonance, the mechanism that forces—or allows—us to adjust reality to our preconceptions. I found this theory extremely helpful in understanding how easily we stay deceived when evidence of the truth is right under our noses.

Ian Tattersall, in conversation and in his books about human evolution, makes it clear for all to see that humans are capable of everything—the good, the bad, and the ugly. That's how we evolved. This broad acceptance of the range of human behavior makes sense of our misbehavior, our shame, and our need to hide bad deeds.

Robert Jay Lifton, in all his work, including studies of Hiroshima and the Nazi doctors, offers a powerful understanding of human resilience in the face of terrible events. He taught me that if you can survive the Holocaust, you can get over a secret, even a terrible one. He also demonstrated how sharing your pain with another person speeds the healing.

Finally, Daniel Kahneman's work, with his friend and colleague Amos Tversky, offers a deeper understanding of how our (sometimes irrational) feelings powerfully influence much of our behavior.

It has been my joy and privilege to serve as an editor for many of the scientists mentioned here. Our conversations about their subjects—and mine—have continued long past the publication of the books, and they enrich my life. I never got to work with Kahneman, but his work has framed my thinking for decades.

It goes without saying that all the errors in this book are mine and mine alone.

About the Author

Jane Isay is the author of two previous books, *Walking on Eggshells*, about parents and their adult children, and *Mom Still Likes You Best*, about adult siblings. As an editor for more than forty years, she discovered Mary Pipher's *Reviving Ophelia*, commissioned Patricia T. O'Conner's best-selling *Woe Is I* and Rachel Simmons's *Odd Girl Out*, and edited such nonfiction classics as *Praying for Sheetrock* and *Friday Night Lights*. She lives in New York City.